# Global Television and Film

# Global Television and Film

## An Introduction to the Economics of the Business

COLIN HOSKINS, STUART McFADYEN
AND ADAM FINN

OXFORD
UNIVERSITY PRESS

# OXFORD
UNIVERSITY PRESS

Great Clarendon Street, Oxford OX2 6DP

Oxford University Press is a department of the University of Oxford.
It furthers the University's objective of excellence in research, scholarship,
and education by publishing worldwide in

Oxford  New York

Athens  Auckland  Bangkok  Bogotá  Buenos Aires  Calcutta
Cape Town  Chennai  Dar es Salaam  Delhi  Florence  Hong Kong  Istanbul
Karachi  Kuala Lumpur  Madrid  Melbourne  Mexico City  Mumbai
Nairobi  Paris  São Paulo  Singapore  Taipei  Tokyo  Toronto  Warsaw

with associated companies in  Berlin  Ibadan

Oxford is a registered trade mark of Oxford University Press
in the UK and in certain other countries

Published in the United States
by Oxford University Press Inc., New York

© Colin Hoskins, Stuart McFadyen, and Adam Finn 1997

The moral rights of the author have been asserted
Database right Oxford University Press (maker)

British Library Cataloguing in Publication Data
Data available

Library of Congress Cataloging in Publication Data
Hoskins, Colin.
Global television and film : an introduction to the economics of
the business / Colin Hoskins, Stuart McFadyen, and Adam Finn.
p.  cm.
Includes bibliographical references and index.
1. Motion pictures—Economic aspects.  2. Television broadcasting—
Economic aspects.  I. McFadyen, Stuart.  II. Finn, Adam, 1946-  .
III. Title.
PN1993.5.A1H67  1997
384.55'1—dc21  97-19752

ISBN 0-19-871148-4
ISBN 0-19-871147-6 (pbk.)

3 5 7 9 10 8 6 4 2

Printed and bound in Great Britain by
Biddles Ltd, Guildford and King's Lynn

*To Sue, Helen, and Becky*

# Preface

This book employs an economic perspective to examine trade, public policy, and business strategy issues in television programming and film. Economists and business scholars have the tools drawn from industrial organization, business policy, and marketing to explain features of trade such as US dominance and the competitive strategies of participants. People with other backgrounds are better equipped to examine the cultural implications of trade. Economics is important in assessing public policy issues. It provides an understanding of markets for media products, it explains the conduct and performance of private sector participants in such markets, and it predicts how participants will react to changes in the regulatory environment.

The contribution of this book is to provide a mainstream microeconomic perspective on a subject area which has long been dominated by academics from other disciplines. Our hope is that our approach will complement the more commonly found treatments of the topic. We stress the uniqueness of cultural products, and our analysis is largely based on their unusual characteristics. We also develop the argument that the economic and cultural development approaches to cultural issues can be largely reconciled.

The book is not country-specific: examples are drawn from around the world. Readers should be equally at home with the text irrespective of whether they are located in the UK, US, Canada, Australia, or elsewhere. The authors themselves, although colleagues at the University of Alberta, in Canada, are natives of three different countries—the UK, Canada and Australia.

We have studied economic and business issues relating to the cultural industries for a number of years, and this book draws extensively on our research. For example, Chapter 4, on reasons for US dominance, draws on Hoskins and Mirus (1988) and Hoskins and McFadyen (1991b); Chapter 5, on export pricing of US television programmes, draws on Hoskins, Mirus, and Rozeboom (1989); Chapter 9, on the role of international co-productions, draws on Hoskins and McFadyen (1993), Hoskins, McFadyen, Finn, and Jackel (1995), and Hoskins, McFadyen, and Finn (1997); Chapter 10, on competitive strategies, draws on Finn, McFadyen, and Hoskins (1995) and ongoing research, and Chapter 11 draws on Finn, Hoskins, McFadyen, and Taylor (1996). We should stress that, although our approach emphasizes economics, the book assumes no prior knowledge of economics and is specifically designed to be comprehensible to the general reader.

We wish to acknowledge the permission granted by FT Media and Tele-coms, the International Institute of Communications, and *Screen Digest* (37 Gower Street, London WC1E 6HH, tel. 44/171/580-2842, fax 44/171/580-0060) to reproduce tables  used in this book. We would also like to thank Edeltraud Martineau for her proficient and cheerful assistance in the final preparation of the manuscript.

C. H.<br>S. McF.<br>A. F.

# Contents

# I

# *Introduction*

Trade in cultural products (especially television programming and film which are the subject of this book) is a particularly sensitive issue. Are cultural goods merely entertainment goods? Why does the US dominate this trade? How important is control of distribution as an explanation for US dominance of feature films? What role does the low US export price for television programmes play? The success of public policy initiatives and firm market strategies depend on the answers to such questions.

To address such issues requires an understanding of how the markets for television programming and for feature films operate. This book provides the reader with an economic examination of important trade issues and their implications for public policy and business strategy. By explaining the economic and cultural characteristics relevant to trade, we hope to provide the reader with the tools necessary to understand the workings of increasingly competitive international markets, and to evaluate international communication issues. The mainstream economics approach we stress has been underrepresented in communications, and complements the more common treatments of the topic area.

## I.I. AN ECONOMICS AND BUSINESS ORIENTATION

Microeconomics examines the behaviour of economic units such as the business firm and the consumer, including how these units interact in markets and industries. It reveals how industries and markets operate and evolve, and how they are affected by industry structure (such as the number of competitors), government policies, and global economic conditions. Microeconomics is relevant to the study of television programme and film production because the 'products' are primarily made for profit and are bought and sold in markets. Cultural products are the output of 'cultural industries'. Economic and business research provides an understanding of why firms behave the way they do and predicts how they will behave in the future. Such an understanding is a prerequisite for effective public policy formulation, as a policy cannot be effective if firms do not respond in the manner anticipated.

Microeconomics encompasses analysis of both positive and normative questions. Positive theory is concerned with explanation and prediction relating to phenomena that can be observed; normative theory is concerned with what ought to be.

The test of a positive theory is whether the explanations and predictions appear to be consistent with the facts. The following are questions about observed phenomena, in the trade of television programmes and films, that we will answer using positive microeconomic theory:

Why are television programmes and films traded so extensively? (Chapter 3)

Why are some product genres much more widely traded than others? (Chapter 3)

Why is piracy so prevalent? (Chapter 3)

Why are regional markets, dominated by regional producers, developing? (Chapter 3)

Why does the US dominate international trade in feature films and television programming? (Chapter 4)

Is the US dominance of this trade sustainable? (Chapters 4 and 11)

Why are the export prices of US programmes so low and why do they vary according to destination? (Chapter 5)

Positive economic theory is based on the assumption that participants act in their own self-interest. For companies, this is usually translated into the assumption that the primary motive is profits. Under very competitive conditions, mere survival dictates that choices between alternative courses of action be decided on the basis of which adds most to profits. Shareholders of widely held companies, be they individuals or institutional investors such as pension funds, are primarily interested in the profitability of their investment rather than cultural or other goals. While managers of widely held companies may wish to pursue their own interests at the expense of shareholders, their ability to do so is limited (see Jensen and Meckling, 1976). More leeway is sometimes possible for a small, closely held company such as an owner-manager operation. The owner-manager will wish to maximize his/her utility (satisfaction), but while his/her utility function may well include aesthetic considerations it will also include ensuring that revenues exceed costs, i.e. that there are profits, as even auteurs like to eat. Thus, although the small film producer may choose a project primarily for artistic reasons, choices between, for example, shooting locations, are likely to be made on an economic, least-cost basis. Even non-profit organizations such as a public broadcaster will, owing to budget limitations, be forced to make many decisions on a benefit–cost basis.

Normative economics considers what ought to be, and often involves trade-offs requiring a value judgement. Economic analysis of normative issues in business or public sector management is the subject matter of managerial economics. Some of the normative questions we will address are:

Should the government intervene to support or protect the production or
    television programmes or films? (Chapter 7)

If intervention is justified, what form should it take? (Chapter 8)

What, if any, should be the role of a public broadcaster? (Chapter 8)

How should a public broadcaster be financed? (Chapter 8)

Should governments oppose US pressures to freer trade in television pro-
    grammes and films? (Chapters 7 and 8)

Should governments encourage international co-productions through nego-
    tiation of bilateral treaties? (Chapter 8)

Should producers pursue international co-productions? (Chapter 9)

How can a film producer reduce the risk associated with developing, pro-
    ducing, and promoting a new film? (Chapter 10)

What form of organization should film or programme producers employ?
    (Chapter 10)

How should organizations that require both creative and business skills to
    function be managed? (Chapter 10)

How should a new film project be developed? (Chapter 10).

## 1.2. CULTURE AND ECONOMICS

Sinclair (1992: 3–4) characterizes the importance of the cultural industries
as follows:

The cultural industries then are those which produce goods or services which
are . . . somehow expressive of the way of life of a society, such as film or television . . . They are industries which give form to social life in sound and image,
words, and pictures. They offer the terms and symbols with which we think and
communicate about patterns of social difference, the aspiration of groups for recognition and identity, the affirmation and challenging of social values and ideals, and
the experience of social change.

Obviously, other industries do not have similar non-economic pretensions
and this leads economists to view people as simply consumers, but, as
Cunningham and Jacka observe (in the context of Australia), 'We are not
simply consumers. We are also citizens in a democratic nation-state with
needs for reliable information and rights to cultural expression' (1996: 68).
Economists need to be cognizant of this.

McQueen, himself an economist, cautions: 'Economists who interest
themselves in the economics of culture normally do so out of a prior interest in culture, and merely make themselves ridiculous if they subsequently
affect to execute a sort of professional troll's dance on the economist's leg
only' (1983: 129). We certainly do not wish to execute a professional troll's
dance. We start with a recognition that television and film are not simply
products like all the others. In fact television and film share three unusual

characteristics. They suffer a cultural discount when traded across international borders; they are joint-consumption goods; and they may have external benefits.

'Joint consumption' means that viewing of a programme or film by one person does not use up the product or detract from the viewing experience, which can be enjoyed by others. In a given market an additional viewer has no effect on cost, while even the replication of an extra copy of the programme to extend reach into another market is very low-cost relative to the original production cost. The same applies to replicating and distributing another copy of a feature film. Joint consumption is described in more detail in Chapter 3.

A cultural discount for traded programmes or films arises because viewers in importing markets generally find it difficult to identify with the way of life, values, history, institutions, myths, and physical environment depicted. Language differences are also an important reason for a cultural discount, as the appeal of viewing is reduced by the need to dub or subtitle and by the difficulty in understanding unfamiliar accents. Cultural discount is covered in Chapter 3.

Television and film may result in 'external benefits', economic terminology indicating benefits to people other than the producer or the viewer. In effect, external benefits can be thought of as positive side-effects resulting from viewing. For example, current affairs, news and documentary programmes, or films may promote a population more informed on national institutions, events, and issues. The external benefits concept, and its implications, is developed fully in Chapter 7.

These characteristics have important implications. If television programmes or films do provide external benefits, the market will not work efficiently because the producers, distributors, and exhibitors who bring the product to market will not receive compensation for the provision of such benefits. Hence government intervention is justified to the extent it compensates for this failure.

The tension between economic and cultural development approaches to examining cultural industries is in part due to misunderstandings; the external benefits concept can be used to reconcile many of the differences. The belief that indigenous programming and films can make viewers better citizens is at the heart of both the economic (external benefits) and 'cultural' arguments. This is not widely appreciated; indeed, the social importance of television and film in promoting citizenship is often listed as a non-economic justification for government intervention. In addition, as we shall see, external benefits is a key concept in assessing trade disputes.

Joint consumption and/or the cultural discount will be seen as key to explaining the volume, composition, and direction of trade flows in programming and film, as well as other features such as the prevalence of piracy.

## 1.3. TRADE AGREEMENTS AND DEBATES

Trade in cultural products has long been controversial. The 1947 General Agreement on Tariffs and Trade (GATT) was primarily concerned with trade in goods, but did include an article permitting nations to impose quotas on feature film imports. Restrictions on television programme trade also became widespread, and the US made an unsuccessful attempt in 1961 to amend GATT to obviate such impediments. Canada succeeded in exempting cultural industries from its Free Trade Agreement (FTA) with the United States in 1988 and fought to maintain this exemption under the North American Free Trade Agreement (NAFTA) (see Hoskins, Finn, and McFadyen, 1996).

The importance of trade issues related to cultural industries became particularly apparent in the closing stages of the Uruguay round of GATT in late 1993 and early 1994. Contrary to expectations, the item that came closest to causing the Uruguay round to fail was not trade in agriculture but trade in cultural goods. The EU wanted to add a cultural specificity clause to the General Agreements on Trade in Services (GATS). Such a clause would have acknowledged 'the unique aspects of culture in the context of trade and would have the effect of exempting cultural products and services from the market access and national treatment provisions of the GATS' (Kessler, 1995: 576–7). The US, on the other hand, was particularly concerned that quotas should not apply to new technologies such as pay-per-view and video-on-demand.

As Acheson and Maule (1996) explain, the treatment of service sectors under the new General Agreement on Trade in Services (GATS) is complicated. Although the audiovisual industries were included under GATS provisions in the Final Act, which came into effect on 1 July 1995, countries can effectively exempt their audiovisual industries from application of most-favoured nation (MFN), market access rules, and national treatment. MFN means that a nation must not discriminate among other members of GATT: all must be treated equally. But GATS permits a nation to exclude selected service sectors. Countries like Australia, Canada, and many of the European nations excluded television and film in order to maintain their bilateral co-production treaties. In contrast, market access rules and national treatment do not apply unless a nation offered them for inclusion. Market access rules relate to a list of non-tariff barriers that are prohibited, while national treatment requires that foreign suppliers be treated in the same way as domestic ones. Countries choosing not to include television and film under access rules were thus able to continue to apply quotas while countries (often the same ones) that did not include the audiovisual sector for national treatment were able to continue to subsidize domestic producers and distributors.

There were reports that Canadian officials advised French officials behind the scenes in the GATT negotiations, and no doubt the Canadian precedent was exploited. President Mitterand declared that the EU had 'the right to ask the American government to have the same regard for Europeans as they do for . . . the Canadians' (Portman, 1993).

Thus, although we are living in a freer trade environment, to the chagrin of the US no officially negotiated move to towards increased freedom of trade in cultural goods has taken place. But the debates over trade in cultural goods associated with the FTA, NAFTA and GATT raised important issues. Are products of the cultural industries merely entertainment goods? Is the US guilty of dumping? Are US distribution practices unfair? Why does the US dominate?

With respect to the first issue, there is a fundamental difference in philosophy. The US does not recognize the existence of cultural industries; instead, it considers them to be entertainment industries producing a commercial product no different from any other. Most other countries regard the products of their own cultural industries as essential to the preservation of their own distinctive values and hence the wellbeing of the nation state. As Maule (1989: 90) explains, 'the position of successive Canadian governments has been that cultural industries are on a par with national defence, education and the judiciary and are vital to the preservation of national identity'.

The French negotiators at the GATT talks accused the US of dumping television programmes and movies and hence practising unfair price competition. Such an allegation has been made before, by Schiller (1969) and others. Dumping is usually defined as selling in a foreign market at a price below that in the domestic market or below production cost. Gordon Ritchie, who negotiated the cultural exemption clause on behalf of Canada in the FTA, when asked about the French accusations, said that the application of dumping to cultural goods was a new development but that 'the dumping argument is one I would muster' (quoted by Conlogue, 1993).

In explaining why the US dominates trade in audiovisual products, the French negotiators at GATT are reported to have stressed the significance of non-tariff barriers to foreigners accessing the US market. In an open letter dated 29 October 1993, sent to US directors Martin Scorsese and Steven Spielberg, a group of European directors posed the question: 'Ask yourself who is really "closing the frontiers" and who is truly "not welcome" in the other's country . . . Do you seriously think that our European films are so bad that they reach only one per cent of the American public?'

The complaints about their failure to access the US market seem to take two tacks. One is that the alleged aversion of US viewers to dubbed versions of European films is just an excuse, and that the US has never given dubbing a chance or attempted to make it work. French stars often dub US films, adding to their box office appeal. Thus Jean-Marie Poiré, director of the recent French hit *Les Visiteurs*, asks, 'Why don't we see great American actors [doing the dubbing]? Why not Dustin Hoffman or Tom Cruise?' The other tack is an 'unfair practices' argument. Alain Terzian, producer of *Les Visiteurs*, states: 'The truth of the matter is that the cartel of large American [film] companies has no desire to see French films succeed in the US market' (quoted by Conlogue, 1993). The specific complaint of the director and producer of *Les Visiteurs* was that their US distributor, Miramax, resisted demands for the simultaneous release of the film in 200 US theatres.

The dispute was not resolved by the Uruguay round of GATT. This was really an agreement not to agree, and to pursue resolution through future negotiations. Article XIX of GATS provides for successive rounds of negotiations at five-yearly intervals, so trade issues in television and film will remain in the public eye.

## 1.4. CONTENTS AND ORGANIZATION OF THE BOOK

Chapter 2 sets out background information on the audiovisual industries and identifies important trends. The relative sizes of the various national markets, and the market shares enjoyed by national productions, are examined. Important industry trends such as the relative decline in public broadcasting, the rise of media conglomerates, and the increasing use of the international co-production mode are identified.

In Chapter 3 the task is to identify and explain the volume of trade in audiovisual products and the composition of this trade. We establish that television programmes, films, and videos are widely traded, and that this trade is dominated by US productions. Some product genres are much more widely traded than others. We explain the volume and composition of trade and other characteristics of trade such as the failure of most transnational satellite services, the growth of regional submarkets within the international television market, and the prevalence of piracy. This chapter expands on two attributes of audiovisual products which are crucial to explaining trade patterns: that they are joint-consumption goods and that they are subject to a cultural discount when traded across borders.

Chapters 4, 5, and 6 examine explanations for US dominance of trade. In Chapter 4 we develop a microeconomic explanation for US dominance of trade in television, film, and video. We consider whether there are underlying reasons why the US would dominate even in the absence of the unfair trading practices that are often alleged. Explanations considered include domestic market size, production in English, characteristics of the US industry and market, and the Hollywood system. The Hollywood studios are distributors as well as producers. Arguments of unfair trade practices are often made on the basis that the US majors use their distribution clout to promote their own feature films and exclude non-US films. Distribution issues are examined in Chapter 5. An examination of the pricing of television programmes is undertaken in Chapter 6. This permits us to evaluate the nature of the allegation of dumping and to question whether US producers are guilty of it. It also provides insights into the operations of the global market for programmes.

In Chapter 7 we consider whether audiovisual products are merely entertainment goods, or whether they are cultural products that are essential to the preservation of a distinctive way of life. In this chapter we develop the concept of external benefits. Whether or not there is indeed market failure of this kind is crucial to assessing most of the trade disputes in which the US argues that regulations and subsidies amount to protectionism and unfair trading. Rationales for government intervention are identified and assessed. This leads us into the subject-matter of Chapter 8, where we consider public policy issues. The case for feature film industry support is examined. Television content quotas, barriers to foreign signals, support of a public broadcaster, and subsidies for television programme production are evaluated. Negotiation of international co-production agreements in film and television is discussed.

In Chapters 9 and 10 we examine business issues. In Chapter 9 the advantages and disadvantages to the producer of selecting an international co-production mode are examined. Evidence on the financial and creative/artistic performance of international co-productions is presented. Chapter 10 examines how best to manage film and television programme production organizations that require business as well as creative skills to compete successfully. The importance of the new product development process and associated marketing strategies adopted is stressed.

In Chapter 11 we assess the implications of the new distribution and production technologies, deregulation, and convergence. We provide an explanation of what the information highway is, and discuss the implications for the television and film markets and US dominance of these markets. What are the threats and opportunities presented for each of the sectors? What are the implications for regulation, public policy, and trade?

# 2

# Industry and Trade Background and Trends

This chapter provides background information on the feature film, television, and video industries. As we shall see, there is no clear delineation between them because feature films appear on television and constitute the bulk of video. Indeed, television and video finance are often key to a film being made. Where possible, we provide data on the overall size of the international market, the size of the various national markets, and the shares enjoyed by national productions. It is important to recognize that in many countries there is little in the way of official statistics for these industries. In this chapter we rely mainly on data generated by *Screen Digest*, a reference source widely used by industry and government. Others, for example the Council of Europe's *Statistical Yearbook 1994–5*, make considerable use of *Screen Digest* data. However, *Screen Digest* itself is careful to note that in some cases its figures should only be regarded as best estimates. *Screen Digest* covers television, film, video, and the new media.

We also describe the industry environment and identify trends and changes in that environment: the changing role of incentives and protection, the evolving technological environment, the increasing problem of piracy, the increase in concentration through the formation of media conglomerates, and the trend to international co-production. Industry-specific matters, such as the crisis in public broadcasting, are covered in the industry background sections.

## 2.1. FEATURE FILMS

### 2.1.1. Exhibition windows for feature films

Feature films are sold in different venues, called exhibition windows, over time. In the usual order of exhibition, these are the cinema, pay-TV (including pay-per-view), video, and free television/general cable channels. The 1992 consumer expenditure per head on films in all windows has been estimated at about $27 for Europe (varying from $8 for Greece to $44 for France), $36 for Japan and $72 for the US (*Screen Digest*, Mar. 1993, p. 60). Overall, cinema box office for these markets accounted for around a 32 per cent share, video 54 per cent, and pay-TV 14 per cent, with the proportions again varying considerably from country to country. The pay-TV share estimate is rough because all expenditures on primarily movie-based pay channels were included as film revenues (even though some include significant non-movie programming), while film revenue derived from other pay channels, free TV and basic cable channels is not included. In Europe there is evidence that the share of pay-TV is increasing, primarily at the expense of video. From 1992 to 1994, pay-TV's share increased from 25 per cent to 32 per cent while video's fell from 39 per cent to 33 per cent. The share of cinema box office fell slightly, from 36 per cent to 35 per cent (*Screen Digest*, Nov. 1995, pp. 249–52). However it is important to recognize that theatrical box office is more significant than market share figures suggest: a successful theatrical release boosts the value of a film in the pay-TV, video, and broadcast television windows.

### 2.1.2. *Cinema exhibition*

As we see from Table 2.1, in terms of the number of feature films made, India leads and is followed by the US and Japan. France, in sixth place, is the most prolific European producer. The average investment per production is given in Table 2.2. As the average US production budget in 1994 was $11.64 million compared to only $0.14 million for India, the US obviously spends, in aggregate, many times more than its nearest rival.

Cinemas are relying more and more on blockbusters as a 'diminishing number of titles are responsible for a growing proportion of the box office' (Media Business School, MEDOC, 1995: 2). The average production budget for Hollywood majors is $34.5 million. Multiple prints of these US blockbusters enable them to be launched simultaneously at a large number of outlets. This blanket launch strategy is supported by heavy advertising, especially on television. Expenditures on prints and promotion for a blockbuster is often nearly as large as its production cost. European and other films are finding it increasingly difficult to compete.

Cinema attendance habits vary considerably. The average American goes to the cinema almost five times a year (a number exceeded in China, India, and Singapore) while the average West European attends less than twice, and a Japanese once (*Screen Digest*, Sept. 1995, pp. 201–8). This makes the US much the largest box office market, the 1994 US box office of $5,390 million dwarfing that of $3,890 million for Western Europe, despite the larger population of the latter.

The extent of US dominance of foreign screens, and how this dominance has been increasing in recent years, can be seen from Table 2.3. In 1992, in the four major markets of Western Europe, the box office share of US films varied from 58 per cent in France to 93 per cent in the UK. A comparison with the equivalent figure for 1985 (1988 in the case of the UK)

TABLE 2.1. Most prolific film-making nations (numbers of films ranked by 1994 output)

|  | | 1990 | 1993 | 1994 |
|---|---|---|---|---|
| 1. | India[a] | 948 | 812 | 499 |
| 2. | USA | 477 | 440 | 420 |
| 3. | Japan | 239 | 238 | 251 |
| 4. | Hong Kong | 247 | | 192 |
| 5. | China | 134 | 154 | 148 |
| 6. | France | 146 | 152 | 115 |
| 7. | Italy | 119 | 106 | 95 |
| 8. | Russian Federation | 300[b] | 137 | 90 |
| 9. | UK | 47 | 60 | 70 |
| 10. | Korea, Republic of (S.) | 116 | 63 | 65 |
| 11. | Germany | 48 | 67 | 57 |
| 12. | Egypt | 64 | 62 | 57 |
| 13. | Mexico | 72 | 40 | 54 |
| 14. | Spain | 42 | 56 | 44 |
| 15. | Indonesia | 110 | 27 | 32 |
| 16. | Taiwan | | 23 | 29 |
| 17. | Australia | 34 | 23 | 29 |
| 18. | Czech Republic | 53 | 18 | 22 |
| 19. | Canada | 42 | 35 | 22 |
| 20. | Poland | 31 | 21 | 20 |

[a] 1994 southern India only.     [b] USSR.

*Source*: *Screen Digest*, June 1995, p. 129.

shows that the US share is increasing in each country. For example, the US market share in France was only 39 per cent in 1985. Inspection of the table also reveals that, during the same period, the market share of national productions has decreased for each European country. In fact it appears that around half of the increase in US share has been at the expense of national productions. This increasing dominance of US films is illustrated by the ratio of shares of US to national films in each country. All the ratios have increased between 1985 (1988 for the UK) and 1992. MEDOC indicates that in ten years (prior to 1993) European cinema attendance fell from 900 million to 550 million. Nearly all of this decrease was at the expense of European films. Thus the problem over this period is not so much the expansion in aggregate demand for US movies but the diminishing attendance for European films.

One question that arises is the extent to which the US market share of box office is simply a reflection of the US share of films exhibited. For example, if 90 per cent of the films shown are from the US, we could not

TABLE 2.2.  Average investment per feature film production

| | 1992 ($m.) | 1993 ($m.) | 1994 ($m.) | | 1992 ($m.) | 1993 ($m.) | 1994 ($m.) |
|---|---|---|---|---|---|---|---|
| Austria | | 2.25 | 0.82 | Bulgaria | 0.79 | 0.37 | 0.15 |
| Belgium | 2.98 | 1.99 | 2.50 | Czech Republic | | 0.52 | 0.53 |
| Denmark | 3.05 | 3.96 | 1.46 | Estonia | 0.31 | | |
| Finland | 0.54 | 0.28 | 0.36 | Poland | 0.34 | 0.16 | 0.14 |
| France | 4.75 | 3.62 | 4.68 | Russian Federation | 0.07 | 0.09 | 0.35 |
| Germany | 2.35 | 2.57 | | Canada | 2.18 | | |
| Greece | | 0.43 | | USA | 8.53 | 9.61 | 11.64 |
| Ireland | | 4.28 | 5.86 | China, PDR | 0.37 | 0.26 | 0.21 |
| Italy | 2.71 | 2.15 | 2.76 | India | | | 0.14 |
| Luxembourg | 0.31 | 0.47 | | Sri Lanka | 0.10 | | |
| Portugal | 0.75 | 0.44 | 0.25 | Turkey | 0.06 | 0.03 | |
| Spain | 1.51 | 1.30 | 1.17 | Taiwan | 0.80 | 0.74 | 0.84 |
| UK | 6.27 | 3.34 | 5.72 | Israel | 0.39 | 0.34 | |
| Iceland | 1.53 | 1.08 | 1.47 | Australia | 1.95 | 1.77 | 3.61 |
| Norway | | 1.93 | 1.28 | New Zealand | 0.55 | 2.30 | 1.40 |

*Source*: *Screen Digest*, June 1995, p. 132.

TABLE 2.3.  Cinema market shares (percentages based on distributors' share of box office revenue)

| | | Origin of films | | Ratio of shares, US/national | Ratio of average US/national admissions per film |
|---|---|---|---|---|---|
| | | US | National | | |
| France | 1992 | 58 | 35 | 1.7 | 2.3 |
| | 1985 | 39 | 44 | 0.9 | 1.1 |
| Germany | 1992 | 83 | 10 | 8.3 | 4.2 |
| | 1985 | 59 | 23 | 2.6 | 1.1 |
| Italy | 1992 | 68 | 24 | 2.8 | 1.7 |
| | 1985 | 49 | 32 | 1.5 | 0.8 |
| UK | 1992 | 93 | 4 | 23.3 | 4.1 |
| | 1988 | 78 | 11 | 7.1 | 2.6 |
| Australia | 1992 | 76 | 9 | 8.4 | 1.7 |
| Japan | 1992 | 55[a] | 45 | 1.2 | – |
| US | 1992 | 98 | – | – | – |

[a] This figure relates to non-Japanese films, most of which would be from the US.

*Source*: *Screen Digest*, Dec. 1993, pp. 273–80.

expect national films to gain a significant box office share. The last column in Table 2.3, which shows the ratio of the average admissions per film for US and national films, gives us some insight into this. In every case the ratio for 1992 is greater than one, indicating that US films are outdrawing national films. For example, for Germany the average box office for a US film was 4.2 times that for a German film. This data does not support the view that national productions are simply being crowded out by US product. Even when national productions are shown, they do less well on average. However, this evidence is not conclusive: it may be that national productions are receiving more limited geographical distribution within their home market or are increasingly restricted to the art house circuit. Certainly there are domestic hits. For example *Les Visiteurs* attracted 13.7 million filmgoers in France in 1993, more than double that for *Jurassic Park*, the runner-up in that year (*Screen Digest*, Sept. 1994, p. 201). *Four Weddings and a Funeral* did well not only in its domestic UK market but also internationally (including in the US).

## 2.2. TELEVISION

Television viewing is the major leisure activity in developed countries. *Screen Digest* (February 1992, p. 37), estimates average viewing of about twenty hours per week based on data for thirty-four countries. Prior to cable and satellite, all television signals were delivered by terrestrial transmission. Only three or four such over-the-air signals were possible given spectrum scarcity. Many countries only had a public broadcaster. Funding of public broadcasters was through licence fees (usually an annual fee per television set or per household and/or parliamentary appropriation (direct government funding)), in some cases supplemented by advertising. Those private networks that existed relied on advertising.

The advent of cable and satellite delivery, which made low cost delivery of large numbers of channels possible, has transformed the situation in recent years. In the hundred largest national television markets, the average number of channels with nationwide reach increased from 3.54 in 1987 to 5.21 in 1991 (a 47 per cent increase). As most of the new channels are private, advertising as a source of finance has increased in importance. By 1991, 94 of the 100 countries had TV advertising, the exceptions being primarily Muslim-dominated Middle Eastern countries. A license fee was a source of finance in 47 countries and 32 employed direct government support. These are not necessarily mutually exclusive categories as 15 countries used both these sources.

Associated with the increase in the number of channels, has been a decline in the ratio of public broadcast channels to the total number of channels. As a consequence, it is not surprising that *Screen Digest* (Oct. 1993, pp. 225–32) finds recent evidence of a 3–4 per cent annual decrease in public broadcasters' audience share. For example, from 1990 to 1992 the share of BBC1 in the UK fell from 38.1 per cent to 33.6 per cent, the share of SVT2/TV2 in Sweden fell from 54 per cent to 36 per cent, the share of RAI1 in Italy fell from 22.7 per cent to 18.9 per cent, and the share of ARD in Germany fell from 30.7 per cent to 21.7 per cent. In Canada, the audience share of the CBC English-language network fell from 23.3 per cent in 1984 to 12.9 per cent in 1994/5, while the CBC French-language network fell from 36.6 per cent to 26.5 per cent in the same period (see Canada, Task Force on Broadcasting Policy, 1986; Mandate Review Committee, 1996).

*Screen Digest* (Feb. 1992, p. 30) estimates (on the basis of data for 75 countries) that the expansion in number of channels has resulted in an average weekly increase of about 40 per cent in hours of programming exhibited. Many of the additional hours are filled with imported programming, much of it from the US. Imported programming accounts for at least half of screen time on approximately three-quarters of the new channels, and for 80 per cent or more for nearly half of the new channels.

The number of television households has been growing steadily, with much of the recent growth occurring in Asia. *Screen Digest* (Mar. 1993, pp. 61–4) estimates that there were 245 million TV households worldwide in 1970, 573 million in 1985, and 725 million in 1992. By 1992, China had the most TV households, 98 million, followed by the US with 94 million. Between 1980 and 1990 the share of the world's TV households accounted for by Western Europe declined from 23 per cent to 20 per cent, North America from 19 per cent to 15 per cent, Eastern Bloc from 23 per cent to 19 per cent, while gains were made by Asia, from 9 per cent to 15 per cent, and Central and South America, from 8 per cent to 12 per cent.

The spread of cable and satellite delivery has been uneven. Almost one-third of West European households receive their television signals via cable or satellite, but penetration rates vary widely. Cable penetration is over 90 per cent in Belgium, Luxemburg, and the Netherlands, but low in countries such as the UK (4 per cent), Italy (0 per cent) and France (5 per cent) (*Screen Digest*, Apr. 1995, pp. 86–8). Satellite penetration is greatest in Germany (14.5 per cent) and the UK (12.4 per cent). There were initially high hopes that satellite would spawn pan-European channels, but differences in language and tastes led to failure in most early attempts. Now most services are targeted at a national audience. By 1993 there were an estimated 129 European satellite or cable channels (*Screen Digest*, May 1993, p. 105). Most of these delivered choices not available terrestrially, although 39 extended the reach of terrestrial channels. Twenty-three of the remaining 90 services were premium or pay services. Three pay services, Canal Plus, BSkyB, and Film Net, are now dominant players. In terms of total revenue, Canal Plus is the leading French broadcaster while BSkyB is the largest UK commercial broadcaster (*Screen Digest*, Nov. 1995, pp. 249–52). The most popular subject-matters for satellite services are general, entertainment, movies and sports (*Screen Digest*, May 1993, p. 105).

In Asia, in terms of penetration rates, cable and satellite are still in their infancy. Cable penetration is highest in Taiwan (38 per cent), China (13 per cent), and India (7 per cent). Satellite penetration is greatest in Taiwan (5.7 per cent), Indonesia (1.9 per cent), and India (1.4 per cent) (*Screen Digest*, Apr. 1994, pp. 81–8). Countries such as China and Singapore prefer cable to direct satellite delivery because it is easier for governments to control content. Murdoch's Star TV, based in Hong Kong, is the main satellite operator, reaching an estimated 42 million homes (*Screen Digest*, Apr. 1994, pp. 81–8). But, as Sinclair (1995) observes, 'although STAR has the technological capacity and access to programming which would enable it to rain down the same service right across Asia, from Beirut to Beijing, this has been found not to make commercial sense'. The reason is that Asian countries vary in language and culture, and this has necessitated a country-by-country approach (in some large culturally diverse countries, a region-by-region approach).

In Latin America it is estimated that cable penetrates 10 per cent of households in Mexico and satellite 8 per cent, in Brazil cable less than 1 per cent and satellite 4 per cent, Argentina cable 45 per cent (but mostly low, 8–10 channel capacity) and satellite negligible, Venezuela 7 per cent cable and 14 per cent satellite, and Chile 5 per cent and under 1 per cent satellite (*Screen Digest*, Dec. 1994, pp. 273–80). Penetration rates are increasing, however, and there has been a big increase in the number of channels. One of the attractions of the Latin American market is that a Spanish-language channel can reach a potential audience of over 300 million, while the addition of Portuguese adds nearly 170 million more. US Spanish-language broadcasters, serving around 20 million Spanish speakers in the US itself, have found expansion into the huge Spanish-language Latin American market very appealing. Thus language is not the barrier to transnational reach that it is in Europe or Asia.

In North America, 68 per cent of TV households in the US and 74 per cent in Canada subscribe to cable. Canada was one of the first countries to introduce cable, the main attraction in the early days (late 1960s to early 1970s) being to improve and extend reception of US border stations.

## 2.3. VIDEO

It is common to consider video as simply another window for distributing feature films to viewers. This is somewhat misleading. Instructional videos are becoming increasingly important, while pornography comprises a significant market niche. Videos of television programmes, such as *Blackadder*, *Monty Python*, and *Anne of Green Gables* are widespread. A recent trend has been to release made-for-video films without theatrical release. An example is *The Return of Jafar*, a sequel to *Aladdin*. *Screen Digest* states that 'while films account for virtually all rentals, they account for a much smaller proportion of the total sell-through market—about 35% in the UK and 30% in the US' (Dec. 1991, p. 275). However, the feature film share of sales of pre-recorded cassettes to the public (sell-through sales) is now increasing because of more realistic pricing.

Video viewing requires ownership of a VCR, although ownership of a VCR does not necessarily imply rental or purchase of videos as the hardware is also used to record and play back television programmes. The worldwide number of VCR households is estimated to exceed 300 million in 1994, about 38 per cent of TV households (*Screen Digest*, Aug. 1995, pp. 177–9). As can be seen from Table 2.4, in seven countries VCR penetration exceeds 70 per cent of TV households, the US having the highest rate at 83 per cent.

Table 2.5 shows that the US also has the largest number of VCR households with 78 million, a total nearly 2.5 times as many as Japan in second place. It is becoming increasingly common for households to have more than one VCR. Japan, where 30 per cent of TV households have a second VCR, leads in this category, followed by the UK (23 per cent), US (22 per

TABLE 2.4. Highest VCR penetration rates of TV homes, 1994 (%)

| | | |
|-----|-------------------------|------|
| 1. | United States | 82.9 |
| 2. | Japan | 77.6 |
| 3. | UK | 74.5 |
| 4. | Bermuda | 73.5 |
| 5. | Bahrain | 71.8 |
| 6. | Sweden | 71.5 |
| 7. | Canada | 70.3 |
| 8. | Australia | 69.8 |
| 9. | New Zealand | 69.8 |
| 10. | Finland | 68.9 |
| 11. | Israel | 68.3 |
| 12. | France | 66.4 |
| 13. | Hong Kong | 65.3 |
| 14. | Germany | 64.6 |
| 15. | Switzerland | 64.5 |
| 16. | Venezuela | 64.5 |
| 17. | Monaco | 63.6 |
| 18. | United Arab Emirates | 63.4 |
| 19. | Denmark | 63.4 |
| 20. | Ireland | 62.8 |

*Source: Screen Digest*, Aug. 1995, p. 177.

TABLE 2.5.  Largest VCR populations by numbers of homes, 1994 (000s)

| | | |
|---|---|---|
| 1. | United States | 78,125 |
| 2. | Japan | 32,066 |
| 3. | Germany | 22,980 |
| 4. | UK | 16,730 |
| 5. | China | 14,810 |
| 6. | France | 14,390 |
| 7. | Brazil | 10,782 |
| 8. | Italy | 9,879 |
| 9. | Canada | 7,810 |
| 10. | Spain | 6,543 |
| 11. | Russia | 6,515 |
| 12. | Korea, Republic of | 5,802 |
| 13. | India | 5,329 |
| 14. | Mexico | 4,088 |
| 15. | Netherlands | 3,834 |
| 16. | Australia | 3,712 |
| 17. | Taiwan | 3,279 |
| 18. | Turkey | 3,062 |
| 19. | Poland | 2,993 |
| 20. | Venezuela | 2,689 |

*Source*: *Screen Digest*, 12 Aug. 1995, p. 178.

cent), Canada (21 per cent) and Australia (20 per cent) (*Screen Digest*, 12 Aug. 1995, p. 178).

The revenue generated globally from rental and purchase of video software has been estimated at $34.3 billion in 1994, up from $28.5 billion in 1991 (*Screen Digest*, 12 Nov. 1995, p. 254). The split between rental and purchase of videos has changed significantly between these dates, with sell-through video accounting for almost all the increase in revenue. In 1991 rental accounted for 70 per cent of the total but by 1994 this proportion was down to 60 per cent. The change has been particularly pronounced in Europe, where rental revenue has declined in absolute as well as relative terms. In the US alone, the first week's sale of *The Lion King* exceeded 20 million cassette units and generated retail revenue of more than $350 million. The push to sell-through has been supported by a change in pricing policy: the retail price for a movie is often less than $20, down from around $80 few years ago.

Casual observation suggests the rental and purchase figures for film are, in many countries, dominated by US movies. Support for this contention is provided by Table 2.6, which shows US distributors dominate the European market. The video distribution arms of the US majors occupy the top

TABLE 2.6. Leading European video distributors, 1994[a]

| Rank | | Share (%) |
|---|---|---|
| 1. | Buena Vista (Disney) | 17.4 |
| 2. | Warner Home Video | 13.8 |
| 3. | CIC Video (MCA) | 11.0 |
| 4. | Columbia TriStar HV | 8.2 |
| 5. | Fox Video | 6.2 |
| 6. | Polygram Video | 5.9 |
| 7. | BBC Video | 3.6 |
| 8. | VCI | 3.0 |
| 9. | Guild | 1.8 |
| 10. | Entertainment in Video | 1.6 |

[a] Based on rental and sales data for 10 countries, excluding France and Germany.

*Source*: *Screen Digest*, May 1995, p. 105.

five positions. In addition, at the retail level, the US firm Blockbuster is gaining a significant presence in many parts of the world.

Piracy, which will be examined in more detail later in this chapter, is a particular problem for video software. Even in a developed economy such as Italy, it is estimated that the counterfeit video market is as large as the legitimate one. In countries such as China and Columbia the counterfeit market swamps the legitimate one.

## 2.4. INCENTIVES AND PROTECTION

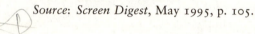

Most nations promote feature film and television programme production through a variety of measures. The three basic approaches are direct subsidy, tax concessions, and quotas or taxes on imports. In recent years there has been a trend, illustrated by countries such as Australia and Canada, away from tax concessions and towards direct subsidy. Some countries, such as France, Norway, Australia and Canada, provide generous direct funding. Other countries, such as Japan, provide little direct funding. Government funding may come from general revenues, as in Australia, or industry-related taxes such as those on television broadcasters or box office admission, as in France.

In some countries with a federal government structure, such as Australia,

Canada, and Germany, subsidies are available from several levels of government. In the US, while the federal government does not provide funding, some states and municipalities do play a role. Often similar funding schemes exist for both film and television. As well as national, there are transnational bodies that subsidize production in Europe. These include the Media Programme, which provides seed money, and Eurimages, which supports co-production and distribution of European film and television projects involving at least three participating countries. The method of allocating subsidies varies. Some are provided automatically to eligible producers, such as is the case for CNC grants in France, while in Canada and Australia, Telefilm Canada and Australian Film Finance Corporation funding respectively has to be applied for on a project-by-project basis.

It is common to protect the national industry through quotas or taxes/levies on imports, with the former being more usual. A quota can take the form of limiting the number (proportion) of foreign productions or requiring a given number (proportion) of national productions. Quotas are very widespread for television programming but less important for cinema exhibition of feature films. Television programme quotas may be accompanied by requirements for specified levels of investment in indigenous programming, often of a particular category such as drama. In some cases such requirements are used to indirectly support national feature film production. For example, Canal Plus, the French pay channel, is required to invest 20 per cent of turnover in new French films.

In most countries television broadcasting is a regulated industry. As well as setting quotas, the regulator normally controls entry into the industry. A licence is required to broadcast terrestrially, operate a cable/satellite channel, or operate a cable/satellite distribution system. Often there are rules restricting the foreign ownership of companies in the industry. While the details differ among countries, the major thrust is to protect national participants and, at least indirectly, promote national programme production.

Although tax incentives are generally less important than they were 10–15 years ago, they are still widespread. The Media Business School (1995) credits the increase in average production budget in Ireland (Europe's highest at $5.5 million in 1993) to a new tax incentive scheme.

## 2.5. THE CHANGING TECHNOLOGICAL ENVIRONMENT

New technologies—including portable compact video cameras for electronic news gathering (ENG), electronic field production units (EFP), digital frame memory, digital video processing, and computer generated video graphics—are reducing costs and increasing reliability. The auto-corrective features of the new digital equipment mean that much less training is required, and a maintenance and repair infrastructure is no longer necessary for successful production. This reduces the barriers of entry into the production industry. The ease of entry is perhaps best illustrated by the recent success of shows like *America's Funniest Home Videos*, based on amateur home videos. Copying of videos is easy and inexpensive. Shipping copies of a video to potential buyers is now almost as easy as the long-established practice of shipping audio tapes. Transcoding from one television standard to another is no longer a problem with the advent of relatively cheap standard converters. Similarly, dubbing costs are down. New standards are on the horizon with the advent of digital, high-definition television.

New delivery technologies include satellite, fibre-optic cable and VCR. The advent of low-powered satellite, where cost of transmission is unaffected by distance, made country-wide distribution of pay and speciality channels feasible. HBO in the US was the first to capitalize successfully on the opportunity this created for satellite-to-cable distribution. Direct broadcast satellite (DBS) signals which can be received by small, relatively inexpensive dishes are now becoming common as the new video digital compression technology increases the channel capacity of satellite transponders up to ten times, and hence greatly increase the choice that can be offered by DBS. Digital compression and fibre optics are also greatly increasing the number of channels that can be carried by a cable system. Within the last fifteen years, ownership of VCRs has increased from close to zero to around 38 per cent of TV households worldwide. This technology has permitted viewers to bypass both the regulated broadcasting sector and the oligopolistic cinema sector and has added to audience fragmentation. Besides providing, as discussed earlier, a further window for producers and distributors of feature films and, to a lesser extent, television programmes, it provides an opportunity for network and channel packagers, including those wishing to access ethnic and other niche markets. In April 1989 the British Broadcasting Corporation began *BBC Video World*, a three-hour compilation of domestic programmes shown in the UK during the previous two weeks. VCRs also provide the viewer with the opportunity to record television programmes and play them back later, fast-forwarding through the commercials and thus reducing the effectiveness of TV as an advertising medium. The ease of video recording has led to a piracy problem, considered in section 2.6.

Cable television is playing an important role in the ongoing convergence of the broadcasting, telecommunications, and computer industries. Digital compression and fibre optics make it easier for cable companies to provide telephone and data services while at the same time making it easier for telecoms to deliver television services. As we shall see in section 2.7, which considers the rise of media conglomerates, convergence is one of the motives driving mergers.

## 2.6. PIRACY

Piracy of intellectual property has been a growing problem. With regard to film and television programmes, video recording technology makes pirating simple and cheap. The United States Trade Representative in the Special 301 Fact Sheet on intellectual property rights for 1996 (US Trade Representative, 1996) provides the best comprehensive source for information on piracy of intellectual property. It singles out China as the site of extensive piracy of intellectual property, particularly copyrighted videos, sound recordings, music, and business and entertainment software. Hong Kong is described as a centre for pirated goods. The piracy problems in Indonesia and Korea are viewed as centring around computer software, while Taiwan is described as having made significant strides in improving the protection of intellectual property.

In Latin America there is widespread piracy in El Salvador and unauthorized retransmission of US satellite programming in Guatemala. Mexico is experiencing significant problems with copyright piracy. Paraguay has increasingly become a piracy centre in South America, particularly in the production of sound recordings and entertainment software. Pirate production centres have been built on the Brazilian and Argentine borders. Paraguay also has become a trans-shipment centre for pirate goods originating in China bound for larger South American markets. Panama has become a major trans-shipment and assembly point for pirated and counterfeited products.

In the Middle East, piracy is widespread in both Bahrain and Oman but has been eliminated in the United Arab Emirates. Boyd (1985) reports that in the Gulf States in the early 1980s pirated versions of the latest episodes of US series such as *Hill Street Blues* and *The A Team* and movies such as *E.T.* were readily available, while a private plane delivered daily tapes of the previous evening's schedule of the BBC. Greece has not yet acted to stop motion picture, software, and sound recording piracy, including widespread unauthorized broadcasts of protected films and TV programmes by unlicensed television stations. In Italy a major impediment to reducing video piracy has been the inadequacy of criminal penalties. In the Russian Federation new laws provide intellectual property rights, but nonexistent enforcement has led to rampant and increasing piracy of US video cassettes, films, music, recordings, books, and computer software.

## 2.7. MEDIA CONGLOMERATES

There has been a pronounced trend towards media concentration in recent years, primarily as a result of mergers and acquisitions. A merger or acquisition makes economic sense if the profitability of the combined company is greater than the sum of the parts because of economies of scope, economies of scale, or increased market power. Economies of scope occur when the total cost of producing different goods within one company is less than the sum of the costs of producing the various goods in separate companies. Economies of scale occur if the average cost of producing one particular good is lower for firms with higher levels of output. If mergers and acquisitions lessen effective competition, the greater monopoly power can be exploited to increase profits. Most countries, however, have laws and regulations aimed at limiting monopoly power.

Acquisitions and mergers between companies at different levels of the industry are usually aimed at gaining access to software or distribution. Expanding into different levels of the same industry is called vertical integration. Examples include the purchases by Japanese hardware producers of Hollywood studios. Sony Corporation acquired Columbia Pictures and Matsushita acquired MCA (Universal). No doubt prominent in Sony's motives was a desire to ensure software for its own hardware standards; software shortages had contributed to Sony's Betamax video standard losing out to the rival VHS standard. However these acquisitions have not been particularly successful, and illustrate the difficulty of expanding into lines of business, and management cultures, with which the acquirer lacks previous experience. Sony, which purchased Columbia Pictures for $3.4 billion in 1989, recently recorded a $2.7 billion write-off on this investment. Matsushita purchased MCA (Universal) for nearly $7 billion in 1990 but sold 80 per cent to Seagram, a Canadian company, for $5.7 billion in 1995. More typically, mergers have been between software providers and distributors/exhibitors. Examples include the $10 billion acquisition of Paramount by Viacom, whose interests include cable systems and extensive international cable/satellite channels (MTV) and Disney's purchase of Miramax, the independent film distributor, and its $19 billion takeover of Capital Cities/ABC, a US TV network.

Some acquisitions serve to expand the company's activities into other media that are competing for the advertising dollar or the consumers' entertainment dollar. Thus Time, traditionally in publishing although it had already spread into cable and satellite, acquired Warner Bros., the Hollywood studio, in 1990 for $14 billion to form Time Warner. Another entity which started life as a publishing company, Murdoch's News Corporation, has expanded into television, notably satellite TV channels such as Star TV based in Hong Kong and BSkyB in the UK, and purchased a Hollywood studio, Twentieth Century Fox, in 1985 for $575 million.

Other acquisitions merely increase a company's presence in the same activity. This is called horizontal integration. In 1987 (prior to its acquisition by Sony) Columbia, a Hollywood major, merged with TriStar Pictures, an independent studio. Such mergers are designed to ensure a sufficient market share to sustain a substantial, and costly, distribution structure.

Some very recent merger activity is related to the convergence between television, telecommunications, and computers, resulting from digital technology. For example, convergence permits cable companies to offer telephone services (about half of UK cable subscribers now use cable for local telephone services) and telecommunications companies to deliver video-on-demand and related television services. The motive to spread risks, by not being totally committed to one method of distribution, has sparked the merger interest between telecommunications companies and cable companies in the US. However, there has been more talk than action, with the planned 1994 $33 billion acquisition of Tele-Communications Inc., the largest US cable television operator, by Bell Atlantic, a regional telephone company, falling through at the last minute. FCC (Federal Communications Commission, the US regulating agency) policy does not permit one company to own both the cable and telephone networks in the same local market, so creation of monopoly power is not a motive.

On occasion strategic alliances substitute for mergers/acquisitions. Strategic alliances are long-term agreements. An example is the 1995 alliance between Seagram Co. Ltd. (majority owner of MCA) and Dream Works SKG, the new studio formed by Steven Spielberg, Jeffrey Katzenberg, and David Geffen. Under the terms of the alliance, MCA obtained key distribution rights to Dream Works' movies, home videos, and music, and rights to use its characters and concepts in MCA theme parks.

Another form of alliance is a temporary cooperative venture, formed to produce a specific film or programme. Where such a venture involves producers from different countries, it is known as an international co-production.

## 2.8. INTERNATIONAL CO-PRODUCTIONS

International co-production has become an increasingly important mode for producing both television programmes and feature films. The term is usually defined to include full co-production, where partners in more than one country are involved creatively, and co-financing, where one partner's primary role is provision of a cash investment. Many countries have negotiated a series of bilateral co-production treaties. France and Canada have been particularly active in negotiating, and producing under, such agreements. Although the terms of the treaties, and their interpretation, vary widely, they often permit co-productions to avoid quotas and to enjoy national status in determining eligibility for subsidies and tax incentives. We provide evidence in Chapter 9 that, irrespective of whether the co-production is undertaken under treaty auspices or not, the major motive is the financial pooling that permits the partners to assemble a large budget. Disadvantages include increased costs and sometimes a need for artistic compromise.

*Co-production International* have assembled a database of 2,000 international co-productions. They conclude that 'co-production increased sharply from the turn of the decade and although the rate of increase slowed, the trend is continuing upwards' (1995, p. 2.1.3). As shown in Table 2.7, *Co-production International* finds the UK and France to be the leading co-producers, followed by the US, Germany, Canada, and Italy. *Screen Digest* (July 1994, p. 155) reports that for Western Europe in 1993 co-productions accounted for 225 of the 578 feature films produced.

The partners in co-productions are usually producers/distributors or broadcasters (including cable/satellite services) who themselves often produce in-house. The main participants are shown in Table 2.8. It will be noticed that the US majors and US networks have not been big players. They have been able to accumulate large budgets without taking the co-production route.

Table 2.9 provides a breakdown of international co-productions by genre. Drama is the most important, followed by documentary. It should be noted that the children's, drama, and animation categories are not mutually exclusive: children's drama of 1.5 per cent is included in both drama and children's, while children's animation of 6.0 per cent is included in both animation and children's.

TABLE 2.7. Country co-production ranking (%)[a]

| | |
|---|---|
| United Kingdom | 15.7 |
| France | 15.6 |
| USA | 13.5 |
| Germany | 10.2 |
| Canada | 6.9 |
| Italy | 6.3 |
| Spain | 3.9 |
| Australia | 3.5 |
| Japan | 3.3 |
| Switzerland | 2.3 |
| Belgium | 2.2 |
| Netherlands | 2.0 |

[a] Ranking is by frequency of country involvement in Co-production International's database of more than 2,000 international co-productions.

*Source*: *Co-production International 1995* (FT Media and Telecoms, London), p. 2.1.3.

TABLE 2.8. Major participants in international co-production

|  | No. of productions |
|---|---|
| BBC | 220 |
| RAI | 126 |
| ITV combined total | 115 |
| US PBS combined total | 110 |
| KirchGruppe | 108 |
| Channel 4 (including Film on Four) | 98 |
| NHK | 83 |
| ZDF | 78 |
| ARD combined total | 75 |
| ARTE | 75 |
| France 2 (including France 2 Cinema) | 73 |
| France 3 (including France 3 Cinema) | 62 |
| TF1 | 60 |
| ÖRF | 56 |
| Canal + (excluding Elipse) | 50 |
| RTVE | 47 |
| ABC Australia | 36 |
| Discovery/Discovery Production | 34 |
| YLE | 34 |
| RTBF | 33 |
| SVT | 32 |
| Lenfilm | 31 |
| South Pacific Pictures | 30 |
| Arts and Entertainment | 30 |
| Turner Broadcasting System/Turner Pictures | 30 |
| Atlantis | 29 |

*Source*: *Co-production International 1995* (FT Media and Telecoms, London), pp. 2.1.1–2.

TABLE 2.9. International co-productions by genre (%)

|  |  |
|---|---|
| Drama | 41.4 |
| Documentary | 24.4 |
| Feature film | 9.3 |
| Children's | 20.9 |
| Animation | 6.7 |

*Source*: Edited version of a table from *Co-production International 1995* (FT Media and Telecoms, London), p. 2.1.3.

## 2.9. SUMMARY

In this chapter we have provided background industry information, including some data on US dominance, described the regulatory and technological environments and how they are changing, and identified trends such as the growing problem of piracy of intellectual property, the relative decline in public broadcasting, and changes in industry organization with the growth of media conglomerates and the rise of international co-production. We shall return to many of these topics in later chapters. The issue of piracy is examined again in the context of trade in Chapter 3. More comprehensive data on US dominance is provided in Chapter 3, while the reasons for US dominance are investigated in Chapters 4, 5, and 6. Regulation is the topic of Chapters 7 and 8, which includes an assessment of the worldwide crisis in public broadcasting. International co-production, as a competitive strategy, is examined in Chapter 9. We return again to issues of vertical and horizontal integration and media conglomerates in Chapters 5 and 10. Further effects of technological developments involving the new media are explored in Chapter 11.

# 3

# Volume and Composition of Trade

In this chapter we first identify the volume of international trade and the composition of this trade. We will see that television programmes, films, and videos are widely traded, and that this trade is dominated by US productions. However, some genres are much more widely traded than others. We then provide explanations for why audiovisual products are so widely traded and why trade is concentrated in certain genres. We also address related issues such as the prevalence of piracy, the rise of regional markets, and the failure of various transnational satellite services. Our explanations rely heavily on two characteristics of audiovisual products: they are joint-consumption goods, and they are subject to a cultural discount when traded internationally. Accordingly, these characteristics are described fully before dealing with the issues. Explanations for why US productions dominate international trade are left to Chapters 4, 5, and 6.

## 3.1. TRADE DATA

Official government statistics are often unreliable, incompatible, or nonexistent, but the data that are available suggest a very extensive trade dominated by the US. Official statistics indicate that, in terms of its contribution to the current account trade balance of the US, the broader entertainment industry is second only to aerospace.

One source of data for the US, Japan, Canada, and a number of European countries is the OECD. Table 3.1 provides OECD data for film and television receipts (exports), payments (imports), and the net trade balance (receipts minus payments) for each country for 1985 and 1992. In 1992 only the US and UK reported a trade surplus. The US surplus was over $2 billion for film rentals only, up fivefold since 1985. The UK surplus was only $25 million, down from $184 million in 1985. In 1992 Germany ran a deficit of over $1 billion, Italy $458 million, Japan $449 million, Canada $32 million, and France $268 million. In every case these deficits were substantially higher than in 1985.

The Institut de l'Audiovisuel et des Télécommunications en Europe (IDATE) has estimated that in 1992 the US enjoyed a surplus in trade for audiovisual products with the EU of $3.4 billion (about 45 per cent

TABLE 3.1.   International trade in films and television programmes (US$ m.)[a]

| | 1992 | | | 1985 | | |
|---|---|---|---|---|---|---|
| | Net | Receipts | Payments | Net | Receipts | Payments |
| US (film rentals only) | 2,031 | 2,115 | 84 | 406 | 478 | 72 |
| Japan (film rentals only) | (449) | – | 449 | (109) | – | 109 |
| Spain (films only) | (75) | 30 | 105 | 13 | 15 | 2 |
| Germany | (1,087) | 74 | 1,161 | (127) | 31 | 157 |
| France | (268) | 632 | 901 | – | – | – |
| UK | 25 | 1,067 | 1,043 | 184 | 434 | 250 |
| Italy | (458) | 235 | 692 | (139) | 50 | 189 |
| Canada | (321) | 167 | 488 | (122) | 19 | 141 |
| Belgium-Luxemburg | (66) | 63 | 129 | (12) | 17 | 29 |
| Denmark | (16) | 5 | 21 | (5) | 2 | 7 |
| Netherlands | (148) | 705 | 853 | (51) | 90 | 141 |

[a] Most countries' data are confined to rentals of cinema and television films. Canadian and Dutch data cover broadcasting, while the UK and Danish figures include production of films. The Canadian data is for 1991 rather than 1992.

*Source*: OECD Services, *Statistics on International Transactions, 1970–1992*, table A.21.


TABLE 3.2.   Trade flows for film and TV programmes between EU and US (1993)

| | US to EU (US$m.) | EU to US (US$m.) | US trade surplus |
|---|---|---|---|
| Feature films | 2,507 | 256 | 2,251 |
| TV programmes | 1,559 | 90 | 1,469 |
| Total | 4,066 | 346 | 3,720 |

*Source*: 'What's Gone Wrong', *Media Business School*, 24 May 1995, p. 2, using IDATE data.


attributable to TV programmes, 32 per cent to video, and 23 per cent to theatrical movie releases)—up $1.4 billion in three years. Most of this jump could be attributed to increased US exports of television programmes to new channels such as the satellite channel BSkyB in the UK. As we see from Table 3.2, the US trade surplus with the EU increased further to $3.7 billion in 1993. US exports to the EU are about ten times greater than imports to the US for feature films and seventeen times greater for television programmes. In aggregate, the trade flow was nearly thirteen times greater.

In 1992 the proportion of film box office accounted for by imports stood at 65 per cent for France , 90 per cent for Germany, 76 per cent for Italy, 96 per cent for the UK, 55 per cent for Japan, and 91 per cent for Australia. As we saw in Chapter 2, the US is overwhelmingly the source of these imported films. Not surprisingly, US features generate more gross box office abroad than at home. In contrast, imported films account for only around 2 per cent of US box office.

In proportional terms, trade in television programming is not so extensive, although it is still very substantial. It is reported that two thirds of the programming shown on EU television channels was European (*Screen Digest*, June 1994, p. 133). As not all the EU programming shown would have been national, we can conclude that over one third is imported. In Canada about half is imported. The recent influx of new channels, often delivered by satellite/cable, is serving to increase the proportion of imports shown because many rely heavily on inexpensive, popular imported programmes in their early years. Several earlier research studies have tracked trade flows for television programming (see e.g. Varis, 1974; 1984; Larson, 1990) and have clearly established that the US dominates a very extensive trade. It is suggested that the US accounts for at least 75 per cent of all television programme exports.

Recent comprehensive data on trade in video tapes is hard to find. As we saw in Chapter 2, video piracy is prevalent in many parts of the world. These unauthorized video recordings of movies and programmes mean that official trade figures, even when they exist, do not tell the full story. Nevertheless, some patterns emerge. The same US movies that dominate domestic box office in so many countries also dominate the movie component of the video rental and sell-through markets. This contention is supported by the finding of Tracey (1993), drawing on the work of Alvarado (1989) and others, that the US is the prime source of video tapes for Australia, UK, Italy, and Spain, and that US distributors make up the top five distributors in Europe. However, video is also used to reach ethnic markets in countries, such as the UK, with significant immigrant populations. For example, one retail outlet in London with a membership of 5,000 is reported to have a list of 30,000 Asian film titles.

Although we have seen that trade is extensive and dominated by US producers, in the case of television programmes and video it is important not to exaggerate the appeal of US programmes or the extent of US dominance. In most countries, English-speaking Canada being an exception in the developed world, domestic programmes attract higher ratings than US imports (see Tracey, 1993 for examples). Audience preferences for domestic programming have meant that most attempts at transnational satellite services have failed. Superchannel, a service offering a mix of BBC and ITV programming from the UK, and Sky both failed to attract a pan-European audience. Sky was only successful when it retreated to target its UK base. Similarly Sinclair (1995: 9) reports:

Thus, although STAR [a satellite service based in Hong Kong] has the technological capacity and access to programming which would enable it to rain down the same service right across Asia, from Beirut to Beijing, this has been found not to make commercial sense . . . a service of this kind is not attractive to the broad audiences it seeks, nor therefore to advertisers.'

Another noteworthy development has been the growth of regional markets where producers based in one country (or more) within the region are more successful than US producers at selling programmes to other countries in the region. We examine these regional markets in more detail in

TABLE 3.3.  Comparison of profiles of imported and domestic programming on ten major West European channels[a]

| | All-channel index | Average profiles (%) | |
|---|---|---|---|
| | | Imports | Domestic |
| *Treatment* | | | |
| Drama | 0.65 | 69.10 | 14.54 |
| Comedy | 0.51 | 12.76 | 4.10 |
| Competition | −0.18 | 6.21 | 8.96 |
| Enrichment | −0.18 | 4.83 | 6.91 |
| Light entertainment | −0.27 | 6.54 | 11.33 |
| Information elaboration | −0.33 | 20.65 | 40.68 |
| Serious entertainment | −0.38 | 0.98 | 2.15 |
| Values | −0.41 | 2.88 | 6.87 |
| Academic | −0.52 | 0.33 | 1.07 |
| Education | −0.58 | 1.78 | 6.78 |
| News | −0.99 | 0.06 | 18.60 |
| *Subject-matter* | | | |
| Crime | 0.78 | 27.25 | 3.43 |
| Conflict | 0.69 | 60.32 | 11.21 |
| Fantasy | 0.58 | 8.80 | 2.33 |
| Transport | 0.56 | 6.97 | 1.94 |
| Relations | 0.47 | 78.33 | 28.52 |
| Environment | 0.40 | 27.26 | 11.63 |
| Health | 0.40 | 11.55 | 4.92 |
| Economic | 0.36 | 23.29 | 10.91 |
| Technical | 0.36 | 5.42 | 2.55 |
| Day-to-day | 0.27 | 33.13 | 19.18 |
| Politics | 0.26 | 11.32 | 6.70 |
| Traditional beliefs | 0.22 | 8.30 | 5.30 |
| Community | 0.03 | 4.00 | 3.74 |
| Welfare | 0.02 | 2.84 | 2.72 |
| Art | −0.06 | 15.10 | 17.05 |
| Sport | −0.11 | 7.44 | 9.37 |
| Games and hobbies | −0.15 | 2.18 | 2.93 |
| Language | −0.32 | 1.04 | 2.02 |

[a] Percentages total greater than 100 due to multiple classification of programmes.

*Source*: Chapman (1987: 17).

Chapter 4, but note here that examples of dominant regional producers include Egypt in the Arab region, Brazil and Mexico in Latin America, and Hong Kong in parts of South-East Asia.

A study by Chapman (1987) provides evidence with respect to the composition of trade in television programmes for ten major TV channels in Western Europe. As we see from Table 3.3, Chapman distinguishes between eleven types of treatment and eighteen categories of subject matter. The table shows, for each treatment and subject matter category, the percentage of all imports accounted for by the category, the percentage of all domestic programmes accounted for by the category, and an index calculated as the percentage of total imports minus the percentage of total domestic programmes divided by the sum of the two percentages. The index thus has a range from 1.00, for a category with only imports, to −1.00 for a category with only domestic programmes, while an index of 0 indicates an equal percentage of both. In terms of treatment matter, drama constitutes 69.10 per cent of imported programming but only 14.54 per cent of domestic programming, giving an index of 0.65. At the other extreme, imported news constituted only 0.06 per cent of imported programming but 18.60 per cent of domestic programming for an index of −0.99. With respect to subject-matter the highest indices are found for crime (0.78), conflict (0.69) and fantasy (0.58) and the lowest for language (−0.32) and games and hobbies (−0.15). It thus appears that the most tradeable type of programming is drama, particularly that dealing with crime, conflict, or fantasy. Casual observation strongly suggests that the same applies to movies for theatrical release.

## 3.2. THE JOINT-CONSUMPTION CHARACTERISTIC

Television programming has the 'public good' attribute of being, in economics jargon, a 'joint-consumption good'. Joint consumption implies that viewers are not rivals in consumption: viewing by one consumer does not use up the product or detract from the enjoyment of other viewers. This is in contrast to a 'private good', such as an apple, where if one person consumes the good no one else can. As a consequence of the joint-consumption characteristic, the cost of supplying a television programme is largely unaffected by the number of viewers. In a given broadcast, cable, or satellite market, an additional viewer for a television programme has no effect on cost. Even where an extra copy or print of the programme is necessary to reach viewers in other markets, the cost of replication and distribution is insignificant compared to the original production cost. Similarly, the cost of replicating and distributing another copy of a feature film or video is very small relative to the original production cost.

Some authors (see Collins et al. 1988; Garnham and Locksley, 1991) have used a Research and Development (R & D) analogy. The production cost of the first copy (or the original) is analogous to R & D, the replication cost is analogous to the cost per unit of the production run. Although the 'R & D' cost is very high, the 'cost per unit' is very low.

The joint-consumption property makes trade very attractive because the revenue generated from foreign markets is obtained at minimal incremental cost. As we shall see in Chapter 6, this also has implications for the pricing of audiovisual exports.

## 3.3. CULTURAL DISCOUNT

A particular television programme, film, or video rooted in one culture, and thus attractive in the home market where viewers share a common knowledge and way of life, will have a diminished appeal elsewhere, as viewers find it difficult to identify with the style, values, beliefs, history, myths, institutions, physical environment, and behavioural patterns. If the programme or film is produced in another language, its appeal will be reduced by the need to employ dubbing or subtitling. Even if the language is the same, accents or idioms may still cause problems. As a consequence, it is common for the French to dub imported Québecois programmes and films into Parisian French. A subtitled version of the British film *Riff Raff*, which had a wide range of UK/Irish regional and ethnic accents, was shown in North American cinemas. No doubt many English-speaking Canadian viewers of the television series *Spender* could also have benefited from subtitles, given their difficulty in understanding the Geordie accent of north-east England. (We suspect the same applies to some viewers in the south of England.)

The sale of the UK satirical puppet show *Spitting Image* to the Netherlands provides an interesting example of the cultural discount. John Lloyd, producer of the programme (quoted by Remington, 1987), observed:

In Holland they have a Dutch puppet that introduces the show. The trouble is there are so many subtitles that you can't actually see any of the puppets. Not only do they have dialogue at the bottom but at the top they have 'This is the Home Secretary and that's kind of like the Interior Minister'.

Obviously a Dutch viewer would have difficulty with the context of such a programme. Just who are the puppets supposed to represent? What is their role in the British political scene? Who are the Dutch equivalents? The subtitles at the top attempt to provide this context, but create their own problems for the viewer. It is not surprising that episodes shown in the US were especially customized to deal with the US political and entertainment scene.

Recent interviews we conducted with some Japanese producers and broadcasters indicated additional factors which they consider add to the discount applicable to Japanese television programming and film in Western markets. They stress that Japanese actors look foreign to Western audiences, who thus find it harder to associate with the story. The highly successful *Mighty Morphin Power Rangers* largely circumvents this problem, as the characters spend much of their time in costume. Animation also minimizes the problem. Another major impediment to trade was thought to be differences in pacing, US audiences being used to a much faster pacing, with more frequent scene changes, than Japanese audiences. Music also poses problems.

US television programmes also find difficulty gaining viewer acceptance in Japan. For example, in 1981 the audience share of *Dallas* was 10 per cent or less, while that of *Oshin*, a Japanese serial drama, was over 50 per cent. Cantor and Cantor (as quoted by Tracey, 1993: 179) have an interesting explanation for this:

In contrast to *Oshin*, the suspense in *Dallas* arises from greed, self-interest, lying and manipulation—behavior that might be considered objectionable and shameful in a culture that prizes loyalty, self-sacrifice and honoring one's obligations. Thus it is possible that shows which do not conform to particular basic values in a culture might be rejected by that culture.

As a result of the diminished appeal, fewer viewers will watch a foreign programme, film, or video than will watch a domestic product of the same type and quality. Hence the value (revenue potential) will be less to the foreign exhibitor/distributor. Hoskins and Mirus (1988) have termed this percentage reduction in value the 'cultural discount' on the foreign programme or film. Thus the cultural discount attached to a given imported programme or film is calculated as:

$$\text{(Value of domestic equivalent} - \text{Value of import)/} \\ \text{(Value of domestic equivalent)}$$

## 3.4. EXPLAINING THE VOLUME AND COMPOSITION OF TRADE

The key to explaining why there is such a large volume of trade is the joint-consumption attribute. As a result of this attribute there is typically a wide discrepancy between the low incremental cost of supplying an audiovisual product to an additional market, which is the cost of replicating and distributing another copy of an existing film/programme/video, and the value (revenue-generating potential) of that product to an exhibitor/distributor in a foreign market, which will be related to the high production cost of 'the first copy'. As a consequence there is a wide range for negotiating a trading price which will look attractive to the exporter, because it is above the cost of supplying, and attractive to the importer, because it is below the revenue generating potential in the destination market.

The cultural discount, when it is significant, however, reduces the revenue-generating potential in the foreign market and hence acts to hinder trade. But the extent of the cultural discount varies with the genre of the product, and this explains why trade is concentrated in a few categories. Action drama typically hurdles cultural barriers (including language) relatively unscathed, and it is not surprising that Chapman (1987) finds it to be the most traded television programme type. Consistent with this is the prevalence of action movies in cinemas. Situation comedy, on the other hand, does not export as well, since national tastes in humour differ and language subtleties are lost in translation. It is pertinent to note here that *Mr Bean*, the internationally successful UK comedy series that has been sold to eighty-two countries, involves virtually no dialogue.

Sometimes the cultural discount is so great that the format of the programme, rather than the programme itself, is exported. For example, Thames Television's *Man About the House* in the UK was developed into *Three's Company* in the US. Grundy Television has made a business of reshooting numerous versions of popular formats using domestic talent. Marques de Melo (1995) reports that telenovela (extended melodramatic series aimed at broad segments of the population) scripts by Brazilian writers are increasingly being sold to other countries, such as Chile, where they are adapted by local writers and produced, directed, and located locally. Similarly, a Dutch independent producer bought eighty *Eastenders* scripts from the BBC, and plans to relocate the series to a location north of Rotterdam (see Tracey and Redal, 1995).

Informative programming, such as national/regional/local news and public affairs programming, is often culture-specific and hence subject to a large discount. This is consistent with Chapman's (1987) finding that news had the highest negative index for the West European channels surveyed. Similarly, very few of the Canadians tuned to US stations are watching US network or local news. However, CNN and the BBC World Service have demonstrated that a significant global market segment is willing to watch foreign-based international news. Also some informative programming, such as nature and wildlife programming, may be universal in appeal. In fact in 1994 the three top-selling (in terms of the number of countries sold to) and five of the fourteen top-selling BBC programme exports were natural history.

There is evidence that the size of cultural discount for US movies is less than for US television programmes. For example, US movies dominate Japanese screens but very few US television programmes are shown. The explanation provided to us by Japanese producers and broadcasters was that going to a movie is an (expensive) event and people go seeking escapism, fantasy, and entertainment, whereas when watching TV they demand fare that relates to their daily lives. US films are perfectly designed to supply the former, but US television programmes cannot supply the latter.


### 3.5. EXPLAINING OTHER FEATURES OF TRADE

Other features of trade noted in this chapter were that, in most countries, US and other imported television programming lags behind domestic programming in the ratings, the failure of most transnational satellite services, the growth of regional television markets, and the prevalance of piracy. All of these features can be explained by one or other of the product characteristics.

The cultural discount explains why audiences in most countries prefer domestic programmes and why transnational satellite services, without customization for different national markets, have in most cases not been a success. The growth of regional television markets, where producers based in a country within the region dominate trade, is because the cultural discount is less for foreign product from within a region than for foreign product from outside the region. Wilkinson (1996: 5) describes these regional markets as cultural-linguistic markets where 'audiences share the same or similar languages as well as intertwined histories and broadly overlapping cultural characteristics'.

The prevalence of piracy is explained by the joint-consumption characteristic. A feature film that cost $30 million to produce can be illegally copied on video cassette at an incremental cost of a few dollars. It can then be sold or rented at a very substantial profit. It is because the product is not used up in consumption and can be replicated at minimal incremental cost that piracy is so remunerative. The attractiveness of piracy, though, will be affected by the ratio of the cost of a legal copy to the cost of an illegal one. Fewer people will participate in an illegal market if this ratio is around 3 to 1 than if it is around 20 to 1. The substantial reduction in price for sell-through videos in recent years can thus, in part, be explained as a move to reduce the attractiveness of piracy.

The joint-consumption characteristic also explains the use of sequential exhibition, noted in Chapter 2, where the same movie is released in cinema, pay-TV, video, and broadcast TV exhibition windows. Each window or market adds revenue at little incremental cost.


### 3.6. SUMMARY

In this chapter we have examined data that shows that audiovisual products are very widely traded, that US productions dominate this trade, and that the trade tends to be concentrated in genres such as action drama. The joint-consumption characteristic was found to be the key to explaining the high volume of trade, while differing levels of cultural discount accounted for concentration on certain genres. Other features of trade, including the prevalence of piracy and the growth of regional markets, were also explained by one or other of these characteristics. We will return to these characteristics. In Chapter 4 we shall see that the cultural discount concept is central to expaining why the presence of the largest national market provides the US with a crucial competitive advantage. In Chapter 6 we shall see that the joint-consumption characteristic is the key to explaining the low level of export prices for US television programmes and to assessing the allegation of dumping.

# 4

# *Why Does the US Dominate Trade?*

Worldwide concern, in both communications and public policy circles, has been with the dominance of trade in television programmes, feature films, and video by producers domiciled in the US. However, some authors question how useful it is to discuss competitive advantage in terms of nation states. For example, Ohmae (1989) argues that political boundaries are no longer of any significance. To illustrate the difficulties, consider the case of Columbia Pictures. Is this a Japanese or US company? It is owned by Sony but its operations continue to be based in the US. Similarly, did MCA (Universal) change from a US to a Japanese and then to a Canadian company when Matsushita bought and then sold its interest to Seagram? Or has MCA remained a US entity throughout?

A solution to this conundrum is suggested by Robert Reich (1990), who contends that the crucial question relevant to national competitiveness is to ask where a company conducts its R & D and other technologically complex activities. It is not where the company has its corporate headquarters or where a majority of its shareholders are domiciled. For television programming, film, and video, what matters is where concept initiation, script writing, and crucial decisions with respect to budget, marketing, and distribution occur, as well as the nationality of at least some of the artistic talent. Hence, to answer the question raised earlier, both Columbia Pictures and MCA should be regarded as US for purposes of analysis. Thus it continues to make sense to discuss competitiveness in national terms and examine US dominance of the audiovisual industry. However, there is one recent development—the increasing use of international co-productions or co-ventures—that is blurring national distinctions. For example, it is questionable whether it even makes sense trying to determine whether the James Bond films or the *Star Wars* trilogy are British or American (Leonard Maltin's *Video Guide* actually classifies the former as British and the latter as American).

Explanations for US dominance considered in this chapter include possession of the largest domestic market, production in English, characteristics of the US industry, and the Hollywood system. We also consider whether the US is likely to be able to sustain its dominance. We introduce the issue of the vertical integration of the Hollywood majors, and consequent control of film distribution, and the issue of the low prices for US programme exports. However, a full treatment of these important topics is left to Chapters 5 and 6 respectively. This chapter draws on Hoskins and Mirus (1988) and Hoskins and McFadyen (1991b).

## 4.1. THE US ADVANTAGE FROM DOMESTIC MARKET SIZE

The US enjoys the unique combination of a large population with a common language and high per capita income, which makes it much the biggest of the world's markets for television programmes, feature films, and videos.

For television programmes, one indicator of the size of a national market is the number of television receivers. But another, perhaps less obvious, is the level of GNP. This is important because it determines the value of a given audience size (to an advertiser or pay channel). From Table 4.1 we see that in 1993 the US possessed well over twice as many television receivers as any other country. In terms of GNP it is also substantially larger than any of its rivals. As we shall see, it is this wealth that helps explain why, in 1989, with 5 per cent of the global television audience, the US was responsible for one third of the world's television programme expenditures (Boddy, 1994).

TABLE 4.1. World's largest television markets, 1993

| | TV receivers (m.) | | GNP (US$ bn.) |
|---|---|---|---|
| | 1993 | 1985 | 1993 |
| US | 210.5 | 190.0 | 6,388 |
| Japan | 77.0 | 70.0 | 3,927 |
| Russia | 55.0 | – | 348 |
| Germany | 45.2 | 25.1 | 1,903 |
| China | 45.0 | 10.0 | 581 |
| India | 36.5 | 10.0 | 263 |
| Brazil | 32.7 | 25.0 | 472 |
| UK | 25.2 | 24.5 | 1,043 |
| Italy | 24.5 | 23.6 | 1,135 |
| France | 23.7 | 21.5 | 1,289 |

*Source*: No. of television receivers from UNESCO, *1995 Statistical Yearbook*, table 9.2. GNP for 1993 is from *Britannica Book of the Year 1996* (Chicago: Encyclopedia Britannica).

TABLE 4.2. World's largest movie markets, 1994: countries with highest gross box office revenue (US$ m.)

| | |
|---|---|
| US | 5,390 |
| Japan | 1,545 |
| France | 795 |
| Germany | 787 |
| UK | 634 |
| Italy | 521 |
| India | 506[a] |
| Indonesia | 444[b] |
| China | 440[b] |

[a] 1993 data.   [b] 1992 data.

*Source*: *Screen Digest*, Sept. 1995, pp. 206–7.

TABLE 4.3. World's largest video markets, 1994: countries with largest video software retail revenue (rental plus purchase) (US$ m.)

| | |
|---|---|
| US | 20,164 |
| Japan | 5,629 |
| UK | 1,755 |
| Canada | 1,568 |
| France | 1,274 |
| Germany | 1,083 |
| Brazil | 674 |
| Australia | 661 |
| Italy | 521 |
| Spain | 396 |

*Source*: *Screen Digest*, May 1995, pp. 105–12; Nov. 1995, pp. 249–52.

The best indicator of size of a movie market is the gross box office revenue. From Table 4.2 we see that the US market is some 3.5 times greater than Japan and 6.8 times greater than France, its two closest rivals.

The retail revenue from pre-taped video cassettes, rental and purchase combined, is given for 1994 in Table 4.3. US retail revenue is about 3.6 times greater than Japan, its nearest rival, and 11.5 times greater than the UK, the country with the third largest market. However, it should be borne in mind that the prevalence of piracy means that the actual market is in some cases much bigger than the official market.

The overwhelming size of the US market does not in itself, however, explain US dominance of the international trade in audiovisual products.

For example, Japan has been successful in building some industries, such as the manufacture of television receivers and video camcorders, on the basis of export sales, notably to the US market. What is to prevent Japan or any other country from doing the same with television programming or feature films? The answer is that a camcorder is culturally neutral. The country of origin does not materially affect the way it works or the satisfaction gained from usage. No characteristic of the product is likely to provide a clue to its Japanese origin (in recent years this is usually even true of the accompanying instruction booklet). The same would certainly not apply to a Japanese television programme or movie, where language and cultural specificity give rise to the cultural discount.

Of course, a cultural discount also applies to the reception of US programmes, films, and video abroad. However, non-American producers trying to reach the US market have smaller home markets and, as a consequence, a discount of comparable magnitude reduces their total revenue by a greater amount than that of the American producer.

The interaction of the cultural discount and market size for a joint-consumption product is at the core of a microeconomic explanation of the competitive advantage bestowed on the country possessing the largest domestic market. Variations of this basic microeconomic model were developed independently by Hoskins and Mirus (1988), Waterman (1988), and Wildman and Siwek (1988). A numerical example illustrates the model. To keep the example simple, assume a world composed of just two countries, the US and Canada, with the US market being eleven times larger. Suppose it costs $1.15 million to produce comparable one-hour drama programmes in both countries and that in the absence of a cultural discount both programmes could recover $1.1 million in the US market and $100,000 in the smaller Canadian market (data presented in Chapter 6 suggests that these prices are in the appropriate range for prime-time drama). If there were no cultural discount then no advantage would be conferred upon the US by its larger domestic market and both programmes would be made, as revenue from the sale of each programme to the two markets would total $1.2 million (in effect this is the situation with a culture-free product such as a camcorder). However, if a cultural discount of, say, 25 per cent applies to a sale in the other country, the revenue earned by the two producers would be as follows:

US producer $\qquad$ $\$1,100,000 + (1 - 0.25)\ 100,000 = \$1,175,000$
Canadian producer $\qquad$ $\$100,000 + (1 - 0.25)\ 1,100,000 = \$925,000$

Assuming that the additional cost of making the programme available in the export market is insignificant, the US production would make a profit of $25,000 while the Canadian producer would make a loss of $225,000. Because of the cultural discount, domestic market size is important; only the US programme would get made.

Another example is provided based on actual export programme price data published by the trade journal *Television Business International*, in *TBI Yearbook 95*, and reflects multiple export opportunities. (For the complete *TBI* listing of prices, see Table 6.1.) *TBI* gives a range of prices (per commercial hour), and in this example we will use the low end of this range, which might apply to, say, a documentary. Consistent with a cultural discount, *TBI* states: 'Amounts quoted are those attainable by producers/distributors who live outside the listed country. Obviously local producers will generally get higher prices from broadcasters' (p. 282). We will again consider the decision faced by a US producer and a Canadian producer considering investment in similar quality one-hour documentaries costing $200,000 to make. We will assume each producer could sell to each other's market and also to ITV in the UK for $20,000, to Germany for $15,000, to France for $8,000, to the Netherlands for $4,000, to Sweden for $3,000, to NHK in Japan for $20,000, to ABC in Australia for $11,000, and to Jamaica for $100. Thus sales in these additional markets total $81,100. The Canadian producer could sell to a US network for $100,000 while the US producer could sell the programme for $12,000 to the CBC English Network in Canada. Assuming that these foreign sales prices represent a 25 per cent cultural discount, the Canadian producer could sell the programme for $16,000 ($12,000 × 1.33) in its domestic market, while the US producer could sell for $133,000 in its domestic market. Including the domestic market, Canadian sales would total $197,000 while US sales would total $226,000. Assuming there are no significant costs associated with incremental sales, since it costs $200,000 to make the programme, the US programme would get made and the Canadian would not.

Another facet of the advantage of large market size is the effect on the optimal production budget. As Wildman and Siwek (1988) have demonstrated, a bigger domestic market leads to a larger budget. As Wildman (1995: 370) explains, 'the larger is the market, the larger is the budget required to reach the point at which a dollar added to the production budget no longer generates at least an extra dollar in expected revenue'.

Let us look at a numerical example in the movie industry. Suppose there are two nations, Australia and the US, with potential movie audiences of 4 million and 60 million respectively. The actual audience will be a percentage of the potential audience, with the percentage depending on the production budget; an increase in budget increases the proportion of the potential audience the film appeals to. With a production budget of $25 million, assume that both an Australian production and a US production would attract 25 per cent of the potential domestic audience and 15 per cent of the potential foreign audience, the difference being due to the cultural discount. If the net revenue to the producer is $3 per moviegoer, the total revenue and profit of each producer is:

| | | |
|---|---|---|
| Australian producer's revenue | $3(4 \times .25 + 60 \times .15)$ | = $30 million |
| Australian producer's profit | $30 - 25$ | = $5 million |
| US producer's revenue | $3(4 \times .15 + 60 \times .25)$ | = $46.8 million |
| US producer's profit | $46.8 - 25$ | = $21.8 million |

So far we have again demonstrated that it is more profitable to produce in the larger market although, in this example both films would be made. However, suppose both producers are considering increasing the production budget to $30 million. Assume that the effect of this $5 million budget increase would be to increase actual audiences in each market by 12 per cent. Revenue would also increase by 12 per cent. Hence revenue and profit for a $30 million production budget are:

| | | |
|---|---|---|
| Australian producer's revenue | $30 + 30(.12)$ | = $33.6 million |
| Australian producer's profit | $33.6 - 30$ | = $3.6 million |
| US producer's revenue | $46.8 + 46.8(.12)$ | = $52.416 million |
| US producer's profit | $52.416 - 30$ | = $22.416 million |

The increase in budget decreases the profit of the Australian producer by $1.4 million but increases the profit of the US producer by $0.616 million. The incremental production budget of $5 million is not worthwhile for the Australian producer because it increases revenue by only $3.6 million but is worthwhile for the US producer as it increases revenue by $5.616 million. A larger production budget will be selected by the producer in the larger market. However, the actual audiences for the two productions are not likely to be independent. Some of the additional moviegoers attracted to the larger budget US production are probably at the expense of the Australian production, which thus attracts lower attendance and reduced profits.

To generalize, the larger US domestic market results in a larger optimal (profit-maximizing) production budget for films and television programmes. This makes it difficult for producers in other countries to compete effectively. While higher budget does not always guarantee greater quality and appeal to consumers, they are positively related.

## 4.2. PRODUCTION IN ENGLISH

US sales are facilitated by the fact that its TV programmes, feature films, and videos are produced in English, in terms of buying power the largest language market in the world. As we see from Table 4.4, the GNP of the English-language market is several times that of the Japanese or German-language markets. Although the number of Mandarin speakers exceeds that of English, this language market ranks only seventh in terms of GNP. Language is an important component of the cultural discount, and hence we would expect English-language producers to enjoy a lower discount when

TABLE 4.4. A comparison of linguistic populations

| Language | 1992 GNP (US$ bn.) | Rank by GNP | No. who speak (m.) | Rank by nos. who speak |
|---|---|---|---|---|
| English | 8,575 | 1 | 489 | 2 |
| Japanese | 3,508 | 2 | 125 | 7 |
| German | 2,480 | 3 | 94 | 10 |
| French | 1,873 | 4 | 115 | 8 |
| Italian | 1,436 | 5 | 59 | 12 |
| Spanish | 1,317 | 6 | 322 | 4 |
| Mandarin | 653 | 7 | 794 | 1 |
| Portuguese | 510 | 8 | 177 | 6 |
| Arabic | 506 | 9 | 202 | 5 |
| Hindi/Urdu | 321 | 10 | 365 | 3 |
| Malay/Indonesian | 223 | 11 | 33 | 13 |
| Bengali[a] | n.a. | n.a. | 115 | 9 |
| Punjabi[a] | n.a. | n.a. | 88 | 11 |

[a] 1992 GNP cannot be calculated for Bengali and Punjabi because they are spoken in regions of India and Pakistan, not in entire countries.

*Source*: Constructed from data contained in *Britannica Book of the Year 1995* (Chicago: Encyclopedia Britannica), pp. 764–9, 778–82, 792–7.

accessing other English-language national markets. In addition, English is the world's major second language, and hence English-language productions are often more acceptable than other foreign-language productions in non-English-language markets.

Of course, US producers are not the only ones with the advantage of shooting in English. Collins (1989) argues that language of production helps explain why the UK and Australia are more successful than would be predicted on the basis of their domestic market size. Historically this has not been true of Canada, although recently this is changing in the case of television programming but not film. Wildman and Siwek (1988) consider language so important that, in their model of trade in film and television programmes, they define markets by language rather than by political boundaries. However, this approach is limited because it does not permit explanation of the differing levels of success of audiovisual products from countries with the same language.

## 4.3. CHARACTERISTICS OF THE US INDUSTRY AND MARKET

Michael Porter, whose strategic planning approach provides an economic explanation of why given nation-based industries dominate world trade, emphasizes that the characteristics of a country's demand and operating environment can be a source of competitive advantage. An optimal environment involves the presence of strong, preferably geographically concentrated, local competition and sophisticated buyers. Such characteristics ensure that the survivors will be formidable competitors in the international marketplace. An additional advantage ensues if the product attributes demanded by the sophisticated (in a business context) domestic buyers lead to product varieties particularly well suited to the world market. Such a domestic demand and operating environment form a desirable 'global platform' (Porter, 1986: 39).

Los Angeles is the single physical location in the world where all the necessary ingredients for a successful feature film are readily accessible—whether they be stars, production skills and infrastructure, directors, financial and distribution expertise, entertainment lawyers, script editors, or the agents who often act as deal-makers. London Economics (1992: 33), suggests that Hollywood's most important feature is the cluster of deal-making activity, and the associated diffusion of knowledge with respect to recent deals struck, record and availability of key personnel, and so on. Proximity, where business and social relationships overlap, also acts as a deterrent to opportunistic behaviour.

The US producers of films and television programmes have long operated in a competitive industry concentrated in Hollywood. In the case of television programmes they sell to US networks, sophisticated and demanding buyers who in the early 1980s had $40 million riding on a single ratings point (Gitlin, 1983). These buyers operate in a melting-pot society that rewards broadly based, popular programming. It should not be surprising that many entertaining, common-denominator, tried-and-tested drama programmes and films that are successful in the competitive, polyglot, US domestic market are also successful in most foreign markets—a sign the cultural discount is relatively small. In effect, 'the format and type of drama originated by the American entertainment industry have in the most recent era created a new universal art form which is claiming something close to a worldwide audience' (Meisel, 1986). Hence US programmes and especially films attract a relatively small cultural discount in most foreign markets.

In the case of television programmes, until recently much of the competition in international markets has been from in-house production by public broadcast monopolies not well versed in producing programmes people want to watch. The lack of competitive commercial orientation in many non-US markets is also reflected in the not infrequent failure to fully exploit a successful series. For example, the British situation comedy *Fawlty Towers*, although very popular, ran for only thirteen episodes in total, and even these were split between 1975 and 1979. As a reading of Gitlin (1983) indicates, this failure to commercially 'milk' a success would never be allowed to occur in the US; as long as the ratings held up, the US network and producer would keep churning out additional episodes even though scriptwriters might be becoming jaded and the artistic quality of the show declining.

In the case of feature films, much of the competition, from countries such as France, is from highly subsidized producers who often appear to cater more to the art circuit than the commercial cinema.

Another feature of the US domestic market is the very high cultural discount applied to imported programmes and films. The evidence suggests that US viewers are unusually insular and intolerant of foreign programming or films, perhaps partially because historically they have been exposed to very little. Renaud and Litman (1985) report that not only will US viewers not accept dubbing or subtitling but also they are averse to British accents. The extent of the cultural discount is shown by Granada's experience in the early 1970s. Granada offered its very successful, long-running (since 1960) soap *Coronation Street* free to any US commercial network that agreed to give it a reasonable trial by keeping it on the air for several months; none of the networks accepted the offer (see *Variety*, Oct. 1986, p. 87).

The limited audiences in the US for those foreign movies that do get theatrical exhibition and foreign programmes that are broadcast suggests that this characteristic of the US market is real, and is not simply used as an excuse to keep out foreign audiovisual product.

## 4.4. THE HOLLYWOOD SYSTEM

We showed earlier why the country with the largest market will find it optimal to employ the highest budgets. In film, the star system and huge promotion budgets have helped the US maintain dominance of movies produced for theatrical exhibition. The significance of large promotion budgets has been enhanced by a change in exhibition pattern away from a gradual roll-out beginning in a few key markets, to a blanket exhibition strategy. This new strategy makes it difficult for non-US films to stay in the cinema long enough for word-of-mouth promotion, important for these films, to be effective. Success at the cinema box office has fuelled demand for the same US films in the video, pay-TV, and broadcast TV markets.

Perhaps the most noteworthy feature of the Hollywood industry is the vertically integrated nature of the major studios; Disney, (MCA) Universal, (Twentieth Century) Fox, Columbia, United Artists MGM, Warner Brothers, and Paramount are distributors, and in some markets exhibitors, as well as producers. Arguments of unfair trade practices are often made on the basis that the US majors use their distribution clout to exclude non-US films (see Guback, 1969). Sometimes emphasis is placed on US majors controlling distribution in the US market and excluding non-US productions from the US market, in other cases US majors' control of distribution within other national markets is emphasized and credited with favouring US productions and excluding domestic and other non-US productions. The implications of vertical integration and use of distribution clout is an important and complex issue, and is examined fully in Chapter 5.

US television, as a result of synergies with the Hollywood movie industry, has benefited from an infrastructure of skilled technicians, actors, worldwide distribution system, and the Hollywood star system. The US was the first country to switch from live television drama to film (an innovation that made export possible in a pre-satellite era) and the first to move from an artisan mode of production, where products are strongly marked by an authorial signature, whether that of director or scriptwriter, to series production in which it hardly makes sense to ask who is the author of *Dallas* (Collins et al., 1988: 56). Now these synergies are increasing, supplemented by direct links arising out of media industry mergers and acquisitions, such as the Time Warner buyout of Turner Broadcasting, and the Disney purchase of ABC.

The US sells television programmes to exhibitors (broadcasters, cable channels, satellite channels, etc.) in other countries at prices below the price for domestic exhibitors as well as below the original production cost. This makes it difficult for producers based elsewhere to compete with US programming in their home market (let alone foreign markets) and has led to allegations of dumping. This issue is examined in detail in Chapter 6.

A controversial issue has been the role of the US government in promoting its film and television industry. This role is central to the media imperialism thesis, introduced by Schiller (1969; 1976) and developed and/or critiqued by Nordenstreng and Varis (1974), Boyd-Barrett (1977), Turnstall (1977), Lee (1980), Mattelart et al. (1984), Lealand (1984), and others. Good summaries of this literature are provided by Sepstrup (1990) and Cunningham and Jackel (1996).

The media imperialism thesis is that, for ideological as well as economic objectives, the US government, in conjunction with the US military industrial complex, pressures foreign governments and institutions to disseminate US films and television programmes that promote the US way of life. This way of life encompasses business norms and political and cultural values, as well as consumption of US consumer goods. As Sepstrup (1990: 5) observes, 'depending on the point of view more, or less, emphasis is given to the "conspiracy" or "intentionality" theory, i.e. that this is a deliberate strategy'. The conspiracy version, in particular, has been falling out of favour (see e.g. Pragnell, 1985; Tracey, 1985; 1988).

Without giving credence to the conspiracy version of the thesis, the role of successive US governments in looking out for the interests of its entertainment industries deserves note. The Motion Picture Export Association of America (MPEAA) was organized in 1945 under the Webb–Pomerene Act. This Act permits US companies to form export associations to allocate customers in foreign markets and to fix prices, terms of trade, and distribution practices such as block booking and blind bidding. (We will return to some of these practices in Chapter 5.) The Act permits US companies to collude in foreign markets in ways which are illegal in the US itself under the Sherman and Clayton Anti-Trust Acts. Jack Valenti, the long-serving President of the Motion Picture Association of America, has enjoyed privileged relations with successive US administrations. The US Government has promoted Hollywood's causes vigorously in bilateral and international trade negotiations, and has used trade sanctions to pressure for copyright adherence. For more on the role of the US Government, see e.g. Guback (1985a), Pendakur (1990), de Grazia (1989), and Wasko (1994: 229–30). However, a word of caution is necessary; the promotional role of the US government is not unique to its film and television industry. For example, export cartels were also set up under the Webb–Pomerene Act in the sulphur, potash, and carbon black industries; and the US government has very vigorously promoted, in trade negotiations, the interests of other US industries such as agriculture, automobiles, and lumber. It is not surprising that it promotes the interest of film and television, one of its major export earners.

## 4.5. HOW SUSTAINABLE IS THE US ADVANTAGE?

In this section we consider whether US dominance is likely to be enduring. In television, it already appears that the domestic size advantage of the US is beginning to erode as market sizes converge and the US audience fragments, and that these trends will continue. However, audience fragmentation elsewhere, notably in Western Europe, will have an offsetting effect.

The high cost of providing transmission coverage and the inability of many households to afford television sets has meant that third world countries such as China and India, despite their huge populations (over 1.2 billion and 900 million respectively), have historically been small markets for television programmes. From Table 4.1 we see that such countries now have large numbers of television receivers. China has 45 million television receivers, up from 10 million in 1984. The number of Indian television receivers increased to 36.5 million from 10 million in a decade, making it the world's sixth largest market. Technical progress has substantially reduced the cost associated with developing a television service. Geostationary satellite transmission is the cheapest and most reliable method for countries with a large geographical area, and costs of satellite transmission have fallen dramatically. Also relevant are innovations in television set design and manufacture. Sets have become much more reliable, a very important consideration in third world countries that lack a service and repair infrastructure. They have also become more powerful and hence able to provide acceptable pictures in fringe areas. In smaller sizes, sets have come onto the market that operate on 12 volts and hence are not dependent on the availability of mains electricity.

The question arises whether China and India, aided by increases in domestic market size, could develop into significant competitors. There are examples of series, such as *Four Generations Under One Roof*, set in Beijing during the Japanese occupation, and *Rajani*, an Indian series following a woman's crusade against corruption, that have been phenomenally popular in their respective domestic markets (Berwanger, 1987: 51–2). However, there is as yet little evidence of export success. Nevertheless, Brazil has already demonstrated how a developing country, with a large population base, can build up a programme production industry that not only pre-empts US programming in its home market but also provides formidable competition in many export markets. The major network, TV Globo, fills 95 per cent of prime time with its own programmes, attracts about 80 million viewers, and earns annual advertising revenue of $0.6 billion, making it the fourth largest network in the world (Marques de Melo, 1990). It made its first export sale in 1975 but now sells to over 130 countries (Marques de Melo, 1995: 322). Besides selling to other Latin American countries and Portugal, Italy has been a major purchaser, and telenovelas have been very successful in markets that include Poland and China. TV Globo has begun to sell to the important German, Spanish, French, and UK markets.

In determining the extent to which development and production costs can be recovered from a domestic sale, not only the size of the domestic market but also the market share available to a particular programme is relevant. In many countries the market share available has been adversely affected by audience fragmentation, and this can be expected to continue. Due to inroads by cable-delivered satellite channels and by independent stations, the US commercial networks have seen their share decrease from 90 per cent for three networks in 1980 to around a 60 per cent share for four networks. Thus an average network show now gets around half the viewers available fifteen or so years earlier. However, similar losses in audience share have been experienced by many networks in Europe and elsewhere as cable and satellite channels have expanded choice.

The multiplication of channels, which will continue with the use of digital compression, has been abetted by political developments. Nowhere has this been more dramatic than in Eastern Europe, where previously closed television and film markets have opened up. One effect is a shortage of programming. The most obvious source remains the US. Cvar (1986: 507–8) has observed that a worldwide trend towards commercialization in an industry often causes one product attribute to assume prime importance. In television the spread of commercialism, and the associated objective of audience maximization, is leading to an increased demand for the entertainment attribute provided by the escapist fiction series. But it is just such 'fast food entertainment' that US producers specialize in producing and in which they already have a well-established brand name.

Although new commercial channels usually find the ready availability and low purchase cost of US programmes to be irresistible, as they mature they sometimes find that the extra audience appeal of domestic programmes results in incremental revenue that outweighs the additional cost. Thus we have Renaud and Dziadul reporting that their survey shows that in some foreign markets, 'Prime time slots that used to ensure high returns to US producers and distributors 10–15 years ago are now virtually a no-go area. In absolute terms, the volume of imports might have increased, but they are used to fill the off-peak period of an ever-extending daily schedule' (1992: 130).

Market growth and increasingly sophisticated production industries associated with a rapidly expanding private sector have also resulted in the establishment of what Porter (1986: 35) calls regional platforms. He has noted that there are often subsystems with significant advantages of concentration and coordination of activities due to factors such as geographical proximity, language, and stage of economic development. As we argued in Chapter 3, this phenomenon can be best described in terms of a lower cultural barrier between nations within the subsystem.

In regional markets the most popular programmes are domestic and regional, with the traditional outside suppliers, such as the US, becoming less important. There is a clearly defined regional market in Latin America where smaller countries import primarily from other Latin American nations, notably Brazil and Mexico, while 'imported US series have become "filler" for the less profitable morning, early afternoon, and very late evening time slots' (Rogers and Antola, 1985: 28). TV Globo of Brazil and Televisa of Mexico in fact dominate not only Latin America but the whole Portuguese/Spanish-speaking world. Similarly, there is an Arab market dominated by Egypt, which exported in 1984–5 an estimated $10 million of programming to other Arab countries (see Berwanger, 1987: 70).

On the other hand, as Sinclair (1995: 2) reports, 'in contrast to the large degree of regional integration in Latin America . . . service providers [such as Murdoch's Star TV satellite service] in Asia have soon found that they have to take account of linguistic and other cultural differences in establishing their markets, which therefore have more of a national than a regional character'. Also, there is no sign of a regional European market developing despite EU encouragement. As Hill argues, 'it is difficult to see what reservoir of common cultural symbols a popular pan-European cinema might draw upon, particularly given the importance of "high art" (both classical and modern) to the prevailing sense of European cultural identity' (1994: 65).

In feature films, Table 4.2 indicates no lessening of the US market size advantage between 1985 and 1994. US productions have increased their market share in most markets. By 1994 US films enjoyed a box office share in Western Europe ranging from 60 per cent (in France) to 95 per cent (in the UK) (*Screen Digest*, Sept. 1995, p. 201). India is the only country to make more films, but in terms of production cost the US dwarfs all others, investing nine times more than France, its nearest rival (*Screen Digest*, June 1995, pp. 129–33). It is difficult to foresee any erosion of the competitive advantage of the US in movies.

### 4.6. SUMMARY

In this chapter we have stressed an economic explanation for US dominance of international trade in audiovisual products. Given the cultural discount, domestic market size provides the US with a crucial competitive advantage. This is accentuated by shooting in English, the English-language market being much the largest in terms of purchasing power and also the world's most important second language. In addition the competitive US audiovisual industry, concentrated in the Hollywood area, with sophisticated and demanding domestic buyers, gives the US the characteristics of a desirable global platform. US pre-eminence in film is abetted by the development of a star system and recently by a move to a blanket exhibition strategy supported by large promotional budgets. The roles played by the vertical integration of the Hollywood studios and the low prices for US television exports were touched upon, but these are the topics for the next two chapters.

With respect to the sustainability of the US competitive advantage, we consider the most likely scenario to be one where sales of US programming will increase in value and volume but nevertheless will constitute a smaller share of an expanding market. The loss of market share will occur primarily because of the continued emergence of regional markets and competition from countries whose size as television markets will begin to reflect their population base. However, in feature films the US competitive advantage is not likely to suffer erosion.

# 5

# Film Distribution

In the United States television and feature films are part of the 'entertainment business'; elsewhere they are 'cultural industries'. Both terms convey the mix of art and business that characterize feature film and television. But, as David Prindle (1993: 4–5) points out, when you have a business that deals in art, firms are faced by high levels of uncertainty. It may be possible to forecast aggregate industry demand fairly accurately, but it is difficult to forecast the demand for any particular work. For example, movie attendance can be forecast but it is very difficult to know in advance whether a particular movie project will succeed or not. A high degree of risk translates into a high rate of failure. As Prindle (1993: 6) observes: 'Most ideas for films never make it to celluloid: The few that are produced often lose money. Most television ideas are never turned into series, and those that are usually do not return for a second season.'

In such a high-risk environment the first order of business must be the development of successful risk-reduction strategies. The Hollywood majors have adopted two key strategies to ensure their long-run survival. One is large-scale operation which permits them to maintain a portfolio of projects at all times. This enables them to offset the many losing projects against the occasional big winner. We examine this in Chapter 10. The second key strategy, our focus here, has been the development of a distribution system which not only ensures that their own product has market access but also provides a stable revenue source.

## 5.1. STRUCTURE OF THE US FILM AND TELEVISION INDUSTRY

Feature films are produced by the seven major Hollywood studios and by hundreds of independents with various types of working arrangement with the majors. What distinguishes the majors and the independents is not just their size. Each major possesses a distribution network in the US and around the world that ensures that its products reach exhibitors and are made available to final consumers everywhere. In this chapter we will explore how the US majors operate their distribution system in order to show why distribution is such a critical factor in their global success.

Feature film producers around the world are in the same situation as US independents—they possess no distribution network to ensure that their product reaches consumers. Such independents sometimes sell completed films outright to the majors (the so-called 'negative pick-ups', because it is the negative of the completed film that is being acquired). Alternatively, the majors may take on distribution of such films on a contract basis. Or, smaller—sometimes national—distributors, or even the producers themselves, may carry out the distribution function.

The average filmgoer knows very little about distribution and the distribution function. In the feature film business, producers rely on distributors to reach exhibitors and final consumers while exhibitors in turn rely on distributors for a steady supply of product attractive to audiences. While one could imagine the hundreds of film producers dealing directly with the thousands of exhibitors around the world, the negotiation and shipping costs would be exorbitant. A major distributor can minimize the transaction costs, ensuring profitability of the system as a whole. As a consequence of organizing and operating this system the distributors are able to capture the lion's share of the profit created. The Americans were the first to recognize the importance of distribution in generating revenues and controlling markets. The early Hollywood dominance of the film industry was not based on favourable production conditions but rather on an early emphasis on distribution and exhibition strategy.

It sometimes seems that US dominance of national cinema markets is a state of nature. But such is not the case. Before the First World War the French and Italians were in a stronger position in export markets. The large US domestic market initially deflected the attention of US firms from export markets:

In the meantime, foreign producing companies, especially the giant Pathé Freres, had already expanded into the international market and had invaded the USA. The great demand created by the nickelodeon boom could only be met by adding imports to the domestic release schedules. (Thompson, 1985: 2)

But the early success of Pathé was itself built on an effective distribution strategy. 'By encouraging local entrepreneurs to open theatres the firm created a demand for Pathé films. Pathé would then open a film exchange in the area, saturate the market and keep other film companies out' (Thompson, 1985: 5). To build a dominant market position American firms had to counter this strong European competition, both at home and abroad. Domestically they attempted to limit imports and to adopt restrictive trading practices; abroad they opened subsidiaries to control distribution of their own product. As Thompson (1985: p. x) argues:

long term American dominance [of foreign markets] came about not only because American firms were able to export more film during the [First World] war itself, but because they instituted new distribution procedures abroad; rather than selling primarily through agents in London, they opened their own offices in a variety of countries . . . by eroding the European film industry's base of support abroad (i.e. their export markets), American competition permanently weakened the strong pre-war European producing countries.

In the US itself, initially, patent control of projection equipment was used to limit competition and risk. Later, market control was exerted through the ownership of large numbers of theatres.

During the 'Golden Age' of the Hollywood studios, in the 1930s, the industry was a mature oligopoly (a small number of large interdependent firms, each controlling a significant share of the market). Each of the majors (at that time Warner Bros., Loews/MGM, Paramount, RKO, and Twentieth Century-Fox) was vertically integrated—controlling all aspects of production, distribution and exhibition. Vertical integration reduced studio risk because in-house product was always guaranteed a minimum market in the studio-owned up-scale theatres; also, non-integrated competitors could be excluded from theatres.

Majors have continued to dominate despite government moves to eliminate vertical integration (with the Paramount Decree of 1949 requiring studios to divest themselves of their theatre assets) and to limit anti-competitive practices such as blind bidding and block booking. Of course, since the Second World War, the industry they dominate has been greatly reduced in size. For instance, US box office receipts in nominal terms (i.e. without adjustment for price change) fell over 43 per cent from $1,692 million in 1946 to $955 million in 1961 (US Dept. of Commerce). The introduction of television and the growth in consumer incomes since the war have been related to this relative decline, but these very forces have opened up new distribution possibilities for the studios.

Prior to 1945 the studios operated on a Fordist basis (i.e. employing industrial mass production methods) and reduced product risk by controlling the market with their strong distribution position. Wyatt (1994: 68) argues: 'The lowered demand for motion pictures, added to the Paramount Case, aided the dissolution of the mature studio system and the movement toward "the package-unit system" of production.' In that system, 'Rather than an individual company containing the source of the labour and materials, the entire industry became the pool for these' (Staiger, 1985: 330). Rather than having a studio like one of Henry Ford's factories, producers maintain a very lean operation, bringing together teams of specialists as needed to perform the various required production functions.

The implications for distribution of these changes in the Hollywood production system, described in more detail in Chapter 10, are usually overlooked. Wyatt (1994: 68–9) points out:

With projects existing on a film-by-film basis, the economic 'cushion' of the studio could no longer offset the downfall created by a risky commercial project.

Accordingly, films with the greatest inherent chance of returning their investment became more significant in this era. . . . After the move to the package-unit system, the studios were no longer vertically integrated; in fact, the studios became primarily distributors of film after this time.

In the early 1960s Universal, Paramount, and Warner were absorbed into large conglomerates while MGM, Columbia and Twentieth Century-Fox remained unaffiliated. Conglomerate control provided the financial depth of resources to be able to shoulder the increasing financial risks associated with a new film making strategy. Wyatt (1994) describes how the majors moved to the 'High Concept film'—characterized by the Hollywood 'look', the 'hook' or star-studded market identifier, and the 'book' or associated products that could be successfully marketed by other divisions of the conglomerate. Although Hollywood blockbusters may appear on the surface to represent big gambles, they really reflect financial conservatism—the pressure to combine financially proven components to enhance the chances of producing a movie with appeal for large audiences. Such films are also appealing to foreign audiences, and the growth in international markets has stimulated their production.

It would be a mistake to think of the Hollywood majors as monolithic constants in the feature film landscape. Not only have there been important ownership changes over the years, with two firms recently falling into foreign hands, but also there has been attrition and large swings in the market shares of particular firms. The changes in market share are shown

TABLE 5.1. Changing shares of the movie market (% of total)

| Company | 1939 | 1949 | 1956 | 1964 | 1972 | 1980 | 1986 | 1990 | 1995 |
|---|---|---|---|---|---|---|---|---|---|
| Columbia (Sony) | 7 | 8 | 9 | 15 | 9 | 14 | 9 | 5 | 13 |
| Fox | 17 | 21 | 18 | 8 | 9 | 16 | 8 | 14 | 8 |
| MGM | 22 | 22 | 17 | 17 | 6 | 7 | 4 | 3 | 6 |
| United Artists | 7 | 4 | 10 | 16 | 9 | | | | |
| Paramount | 14 | 14 | 13 | 17 | 22 | 16 | 22 | 15 | 10 |
| Universal | 7 | 7 | 10 | 12 | 5 | 20 | 9 | 14 | 13 |
| Warner Bros. | 14 | 11 | 15 | 6 | 18 | 14 | 12 | 13 | 16 |
| RKO | 9 | 9 | 4 | | | | | | |
| Disney/Buena Vista | 1 | 1 | 1 | 9 | 5 | 4 | 10 | 16 | 19 |
| Others | 4 | 3 | 3 | 1 | 16 | 9 | 25 | 20 | 15 |

*Source*: J. W. Finler, *The Hollywood Story* (London: Mandarin, 1992), p. 52; Standard and Poor's Industry Surveys, *Leisure Time*, 1 (18 Apr. 1996), p. L27.

in Table 5.1. As well as the majors there are hundreds of US independent film and television production companies with productions to be distributed and exhibited. Sometimes the US independents sell all rights to completed films to one of the majors in what is termed a 'negative pick-up'; sometimes they negotiate a distribution deal with one of the majors or some smaller distributor; sometimes they distribute on their own. Non-US producers have similar options, but in their case the smaller distributor might be one based in their home country. A theatrical film passes from the producer to one of these distributors and is then rented to exhibitors in each country.

Until the 1950s all exhibition took place in theatres. Subsequent technological advance, however, has created new exhibition windows—video, pay-per-view television, network television, and basic cable—in each market. The distribution in these other windows is, however, patterned on the feature film model, with the Hollywood majors playing a dominant role. The basic economic rationale behind this is the desire by the distributor of the feature film to capitalize as much as possible on the marketing and promotional activities undertaken for the feature film.

The distributor–exhibitor relationship is one of mutual dependence: the distributors need exhibitors to provide venues so that films can be seen by audiences, while exhibitors need distributors to provide them with a steady stream of good films to maintain the viability of their theatres. Donahue (1987: 99–142) provides a detailed analysis of this relationship. This mutual dependence is an important motivation for vertical integration in the feature film industry. Ever since the Paramount decree forced the majors to divest themselves of their theatre holdings there has been conflict between distributors and exhibitors. Also, conflict between independent producers and the majors has occurred. Prindle (1993: 17) notes:

Independents accuse the majors of being too lacking in vision to recognize the merit in their films (and therefore refusing to distribute them) or having distributed them, of marketing them incompetently so that they do not make money; or having distributed and marketed them well so that they generate a great deal of revenue, of cheating them out of their just share of the profits.

These same concerns are often voiced by non-US producers, seemingly little aware that the distribution power of the Hollywood majors affects all production companies without distribution capability regardless of nationality.

Two trade practices, used by distributors to lessen their risks, are block booking and blind bidding. Block booking occurs when exhibitors are required to take a group of films, including a number of films they would not normally choose to exhibit, in order to secure rights to some other film that is believed to have high market potential. Blind bidding occurs when exhibitors are required to bid on forthcoming films before they are available for viewing. Despite being outlawed in over twenty US states these practices continue because they provide a method of market control for distributors and security of supply for exhibitors.

## 5.2. THE IMPORTANCE OF FILM DISTRIBUTORS AS PROVIDERS OF INFORMATION

A feature film is a product that consumers must pay for before they know how much enjoyment they will receive. Attending large numbers of other films provides little guidance in choosing a new movie. Seeing the film once to become informed and then returning to the theatre is no solution to this problem, since the enjoyment of the second viewing would be much reduced. In other words, search activity and experience, which are valuable to consumers for many other products, are of little guidance to consumers in choosing which movie to attend. This causes a fundamental difficulty for the feature film business because, if product quality cannot be communicated, then producers have an incentive to produce shoddy products and consumers have an incentive to buy little since they are never aware of truly enjoyable offerings.

There are two general ways of getting around this problem. One is the use of reputation as a proxy for quality. Another is for consumers to rely on alternative sources of information about a product such as research, consumer reports, advice from friends, and advertising. In the case of features the main pieces of information required by consumers (aside from exhibition venue information) are: first, the target audience of the film and second, the quality of the film. Film reviews and advice from friends (word of mouth) can help on both scores, but the distributor who deals with trailers, promotion, and the advertising campaign plays a critical role.

London Economics (1992: 11–13) provides an insightful analysis of the distributor's role. When the Hollywood majors first became dominant the studio name alone was used as a method of quality certification. Later the branding switched to the creative personnel—the star system. 'Stars established the value of motion pictures as a marketable commodity. In economic terms, stars by virtue of their unique appeal and drawing power stabilized rental prices and guaranteed companies operated at a profit' (Klaprat, 1985: 131). Sequels work on the reputation dimension in another way—consumers satisfied with earlier episodes will use the reputation of these episodes as a guide to attending the sequel. Advertising budgets of releases by the majors now average well over $10 million, but with good reason. Advertising can not only convey the target audience of the film but also, by its very existence, provide consumers with a proxy measure of quality. A big advertising campaign means that knowledgeable people in the business believe the advertised movie to be a quality product; consumers can take this into account in deciding on which films to attend. We examine the star system, sequels, and advertising and promotion further in Chapter 10.

Just as information provided by the distributor influences consumer decision-making, it should be no surprise to find that it is also very important in influencing production decisions in the independent film sector. The backing of a distributor is an important element in obtaining financing for an independent film for two reasons: it shows that those expert in such matters are supportive and it also gives assurance that the film will be distributed. But how do distributors decide which films they should be involved with? If they are profit-oriented businesses they will want to be distributing the films that will attract big audiences. Therefore the same factors that influence the decisions of audiences to attend the showing of a movie (discussed above) will be the factors that will influence the distributor's decision.

London Economics (1992: 13) caricatures these self-reinforcing tendencies:

consumers watch films which are well promoted and feature big names: distributors and financiers direct their finance and efforts to well promoted films with big names . . . success breeds success in this industry . . . films are cut to fit the cloth they have, but the cloth they have matches the size of the cut they are expected to make.

Distributors are responsible for advertising, promotion and branding. They decide on the release pattern which also conveys quality signals to consumers (a wide release is a big gamble on a marginal film); similarly for the type of theatre booked (prestige locations in major markets are a vote of confidence). Through all of these tools the distributor builds awareness and 'want-to-see' for the film. In addition the distributor must ensure that the film is available in suitable venues. But it is this control over the flow of information to both sources of finance and consumers that gives the distributor such a central role in independent film-making.

## 5.3. DISTRIBUTION: HOW DOES IT WORK?

With marketing and distribution budgets of $50 million for some recent Hollywood blockbusters, it is obvious that distribution costs play an important role in the overall financial success of a film. But what is behind these big figures? Let us take a look at how a typical distribution deal is set up and then examine the implications of such a setup for the independent film producer.

Goldberg (1991: 169–70) provides an excellent description of the typical 90:10 percentage deal. Consumers pay the exhibitor in order to view the film. The total of all ticket sales for the film is termed its 'box office gross'.

Exhibitors, in order to obtain the right to exhibit the film, must agree to give the distributor a share of the box office gross. In the 1990s most films, especially those from the majors, have been sold on the basis of a 90:10 sharing of the box-office gross. The distributors take 90 per cent of the box-office gross, the exhibitors retaining 10 per cent. This is not as unfavourable to the exhibitors as it appears on the surface, since the exhibitors first deduct the house expenses, called the 'nut', from the gross before calculating the distributor's share. Goldberg provides the following example:

| | |
|---|---|
| Box-office gross for one week | $10,000 |
| House expenses | −3,000 |
| Net gross | 7,000 |
| Exhibitor's share (10%) | 700 |
| Distributor's share (90%) | 6,300 |

The 90:10 deal generally specifies floors or minimum percentages each week. For example, a contract may specify that the distributor will receive 90% of the net gross after house expenses are deducted or 70% of the box office gross before house expenses, whichever is higher. If you apply this to the example described above, the distributor would receive $7,000 or 70% of the theatre gross, instead of $6,300 or 90% of the net gross after the nut is deducted. The floors are generally specified for the entire run. For example, a contract for an exclusive run might require 90:10 over house expenses of $3,000, with minimum terms as follows: Week 1, 70%; Week 2, 70%; Week 3, 60%; Week 4, 60%; Week 5, 50%; Week 6, 50%; Week 7, 40%; Week 8, 40%. In other words, for each week of the engagement, the theatre will owe the distributor 90% of the net gross after deduction of the house expenses or 70, 60, 50, or 40% of the box-office gross—whichever is higher.

The exact terms agreed upon depend on the quality of the film and the relationship between the distributor and the exhibitor. The Hollywood majors with their continuing stream of desirable product and their strong market position do not have to enter into weak agreements or allow adjustments. Their position is that if exhibitors want access to their films they must honour the standard contract.

Looking at distributor–exhibitor relations in this way may lead the reader to sympathize with the plight of the exhibitor, forced to subsist on a small fraction of the gross revenues his/her theatre generates because of a necessarily unfavourable bargain with powerful distributors. But exhibitors have some flexibility in calculating the expenses taken off the top, and they keep all of the concession revenues (which can be very substantial). And, in any event, the less distributors and exhibitors retain of gross revenues the more left for creators. But is this really true? How does box office revenue translate into money in the pockets of producers?

The *Economist* (10 May 1986) provides a nice example. Assuming the exhibitor's house expenses (the nut) to be 10 per cent of box office gross, if a standard 90:10 split agreement is in place the distributor will collect 81 cents in the dollar as rentals. But this 81 cents is not passed on to the producer. Thirty per cent of rentals goes to the distributor as a distribution fee (say 24 cents on the dollar). Advertising and promotion of the film will account for somewhere in the neighbourhood of 25 per cent of rentals (another 20 cents), leaving only 37 cents. If prints, taxes, and transportation account for 5 cents and recoupment of negative costs 30 cents, there are only 2 cents in the dollar left for profit. Even this two cents may have to be split with the studio if they have provided up-front financing of some kind. If leading actors possess sufficient star appeal to have negotiated 'points' or participation in the original gross rentals of 81 cents, then the producer will end up in the hole.

Before proceeding we should note one important caveat. It is true that independent producers have difficulty generating profits on projects. But there is no shortage of producers. Why? Many producers produce not for profit but for fees. Their remuneration comes from the (at times quite generous) producer's fees built into the project budget. Even if the project recoups nothing for the investors and the public agencies putting money into it, the producer may pocket all that he/she ever expected to from the project—their production fee. The incentive implications of this for an independent production industry reliant on public funding are clear. Financial discipline, imposed by the market, forces Hollywood creators to tailor their films to the desires of the moviegoing public; independent producers able to draw on public funds are much better placed to pursue artistic and creative agendas unrelated to what moviegoers wish to see.

The key to survival is skilful foreign distribution. The Hollywood majors offer the safest approach, but it is a high-cost solution. They have a strong distribution infrastructure worldwide and are able to include independently produced product in their block-booking packages. But the majors charge hefty distribution fees (30–40 per cent of rentals) and incur large promotion and marketing costs. Also, cross-collateralizing projects may mean that big gains for a project in some countries may be offset against losses in other countries. Alternatively, the producer can negotiate market by market, often with a local distributor who will charge a lower distribution fee. Cross-collateralization is avoided, but the lower fee reflects a lower level of marketplace clout, and perhaps even exclusion from the best play-dates and venues. A third possibility is to split off the various types of rights (cinema, pay-TV, basic cable, and video) and make separate deals for each.

The processes of subdividing the rights bundle by technology and dealing with independent distributors in each geographical market share a fundamental shortcoming. Since the owners of the rights for each technology or for each market do not possess world rights, they adopt a limited (i.e. limited to their technology or their geographical area) perspective in their promotional activities. Only the majors can spend big with the hope of generating revenue all along the value chain as a result of their efforts.

## 5.4. THE POLITICAL ECONOMY OF FEATURE FILM DISTRIBUTION

In countries other than the US, where domestic feature films account for low and declining percentages of cinema screen time, film distribution has long been of particular public policy interest. The concern in these countries is that feature film distribution is dominated by the American firms, and moreover, that these American firms exert market power. The worry is that this situation limits the role of domestic distributors, with the overall result that domestic feature films cannot reach an audience even in their country of origin.

Not unsurprisingly, this argument has been made most forcefully in Canada where the Canadian feature film market is so closely integrated with that of the US that all box office and trade data reflect the North American market as a whole. Pendakur (1982: 360), for instance, concludes:

> The monopolistic system of distribution and exhibition in Canada, and its adverse impact on unintegrated Canadian-owned companies in distribution and production, has developed over the last sixty years only to the mutual advantage of the major US distribution corporations and their affiliated circuits in Canada. Assured profits for both these parties is the main goal of these relationships. Underdevelopment in the indigenously controlled production/distribution sector is perpetuated by lack of participation for Canadian capital in production, lack of access for Canadian films to Canadian screens, nonavailability of the best playing dates, and extraction of profits by the American majors without any significant investment in Canadian feature films.

Let us examine the two elements of the argument in turn.

### 5.4.1. *Those damn Americans*

Probably the easiest issue to get out of the way is the question of the nationality of the Hollywood majors. Independent producers outside the US may feel they are at the mercy of the majors, but there is little reason to see this as a plot against foreign independents by US majors. As the previous discussion attempted to make clear, independent producers in the US itself are subject to these very same pressures. In both instances the basic economic driving forces of the industry draw the majors into a pattern of behaviour designed to control risk in an industry characterized by high levels of uncertainty.

In the European context the Media Business School (1995: 6) indeed credits the Hollywood majors with identifying a marketing strategy that the Europeans themselves should adopt:

> A Single European Market exists only for American films largely because European distributors have concentrated solely on domestic markets. The US majors approach

to Europe as a homogenous market has further consolidated their strength. Their success mocks the notion that Europe's linguistic and cultural diversity must limit the potential for European films to cross borders.

### 5.4.2. *What about the market power of the Hollywood majors?*

So the Hollywood majors exert damaging levels of market power in feature film markets throughout the world? They are certainly the dominant players. For example, in European countries in 1991 the distribution arms of the majors accounted for an average of 72.5 per cent of box office revenues (Pham and Watson, 1993: 83). Were they available, figures for Canada would be even higher. A number of reports prepared by and for the Canadian government (Stratavision, 1985; Canada, Task Force on Film Distribution . . . , 1983; Canada, Film Industry Task Force, 1985) have argued that the dominant market position of the Hollywood majors is a result of their vertical integration and anti-competitive practices. The dominant US majors are able to foreclose opportunities for domestic productions which convey national cultural values: the classic case of market concentration leading to poor economic performance in an industry. But, as Globerman and Vining (1987) point out, there is more to market structure than concentration. For example, the few firms accounting for a high percentage of industry sales will have little ability to exploit their situation if they are threatened by potential entry.

So what are the barriers to the entry of new competitors in the feature film distribution business? The majors do not control production techniques; they do not have a monopoly on inputs; the supply of capital to enter the business is not restricted by them. A product differentiation barrier exists in the sense that the majors enjoy an 'accumulative preference' by consumers for their products. But this is a weak barrier to entry: the barrier will disappear if the majors falter in their ability to continue to deliver the types of film that appeal to audiences. Entrants also have the option of producing such products in competition with the majors. Some see the vertical integration of the Hollywood majors as a barrier to the entry of new competitors, but if market power exists at one level of an industry then there is usually little reason to integrate to another stage to realize the gains from monopoly power. In this instance there is little reason to think that the majors control the acquisition policy of the exhibitors. 'If anything, the distributors are subject to the exercise of market power on the part of exhibitors and not vice versa' (Globerman and Vining, 1987: p. xix). We have seen above that big sums of money are involved in the worldwide distribution of a feature film and that the risks are high; these factors do create a scale economy barrier to the entry of new film distribution firms.

In short, there is a degree of concentration in the feature film distribution industry and there is an economies-of-scale barrier to the entry of new competitors. The crucial question is whether this structure has remained workably competitive; whether film distribution remains a contestable market. Globerman and Vining (1987: p. xx) conclude that it has, noting the continued entry of new domestic film distributors and the opening up of new ancillary markets (exhibition windows).


## 5.5. WHAT'S GONE WRONG WITH THE FEATURE FILM BUSINESS OUTSIDE THE US?

The world market for audiovisual products—film, television, and various new media—is growing at explosive rates. Theatrical release of feature films is becoming a smaller and smaller proportion of this business each year, but nevertheless features remain central because they so often function as the locomotive that pulls the rest of the audiovisual train. Features have big budgets; they showcase the stars and attract the attention that moves the product profitably through the various exhibition windows. But the industry worldwide is each year becoming more and more dominated by the US majors.

In 1965, 60 per cent of the films exhibited in Europe were European, with 35 per cent from the US. By 1995 the European share of its own market had fallen to 20 per cent, with nearly all the remainder accounted for by US films. Market share data for each of the eleven EU countries in 1992, is shown in Table 5.2. France has the highest domestic market share at 35 per cent, but even this is dwarfed by the US share of 58 per cent. Most of the European share in each country is accounted for by domestic

TABLE 5.2. Box office share of US, domestic, EU, and other films in European markets, 1992 (%)

|  | US | Domestic | Other Europe | Other |
|---|---|---|---|---|
| France | 58 | 35 | 4 | 3 |
| Italy | 74 | 19 | 6 | 1 |
| Germany | 83 | 10 | 6 | 1 |
| Spain | 69 | 10 | 20 | 1 |
| UK | 84 | 14 | 2 | 5 |
| Holland | 78 | 13 | 3 | 6 |
| Belgium | 79 | 3 | 16 | 2 |
| Denmark | 74 | 18 | 4 | 2 |
| Greece | 92 | 2 | 3 | 2 |
| Portugal | 85 | 1 | 9 | 5 |
| Ireland | 88 | 8 | 4 | 0 |

*Source*: 'What's Gone Wrong?', *Media Business School* (1995), p. 2.

product; there is very limited intra-European film trade. As in North America, a small number of titles account for a large percentage of the box office. The Hollywood blockbusters with their heavy marketing support have carried the day. Production and distribution companies operating at the national level cannot achieve the scale required for commercial success. National fragmentation, although desirable for cultural reasons, hamstrings the competitive potential of such firms. They cannot achieve the scale of operation necessary to compete in the global marketplace.

## 5.6. THE STRUCTURE OF FILM DISTRIBUTION IN EUROPE

Pham and Watson (1993) provide a very helpful description of the structure of the film industry in Europe. The majors capture over 70 per cent of the European box office with 20–35 releases annually (some of which are negative pick-ups). In the US these same releases will account for the lion's share of the box office every year. The distribution structure of the majors is even more concentrated than it is in the US since Paramount, Universal (originally called Universal, then MCA, and now back to Universal) and MGM have formed a joint venture, United International Pictures, to distribute their films overseas. Columbia (Sony), Fox, Warner, and Disney, however, each handle their own pictures. Most other films are released by a handful of local distributors that release between 10 and 30 films per year. The largest of these domestic distributors usually have output deals (or some informal alliance) with one or more local producers and several international sales agencies. The output deal gives the distributor rights to a number of pictures over some specified time period.

The output deal serves to reduce the business risk of both the independent domestic producer and the independent distributor. The former is assured of a distribution channel for its product and the latter is assured of a supply of product to enable it to carry on business and bear corporate overheads. As in the US, the profits from a few successful films must more than offset the losses of the numerous box office failures if a distributor is to remain in business in the long run. Of course, in Hollywood this is the accounting equivalent of moving money from one pocket to another. The problem for the independent distributors dealing with a number of independent producers is that the pockets are on different pairs of trousers/pants: the producers of unprofitable projects are willing to be supported by the gains on successful projects, but the converse is not true.

In addition to the major distributors and the large domestic distributors there are, in each country, a number of small distributors specializing in art-house films and re-releases. In France and Germany these firms are numerous and very small—handling only one or two films a year. In Britain there has been competitive consolidation and these niche operators are larger.

As in other parts of the world, this distribution apparatus hobbles non-Hollywood-major films in the battle for screen time. MEDOC (Media Business School, 1995: 3–4) concludes:

The absence of a European distribution network dooms European films to an increasingly domestic career and puts a halt to any effort to create a European industry and a European market. As long ago as 1968 when European cinema was in the ascendancy, European distributors were perceived as being 'too fragmented, too closely limited to regional frameworks'. There's now a greater reliance on public subsidy within each European territory but this assistance is rarely used for anything other than sustaining ailing domestic policies . . . On a transnational scale any sort of political strategy or worldwide distribution structure has been absent, leaving the field uncontested to US majors. Europe lacks powerful companies with resources to operate global distribution from a unified position and to amass the huge catalogues which the US majors use as capital assets. An estimated 900 distribution companies struggle to distribute 500 films a year.

The Media Business School argues that consolidation of the many small distributors is critical, since it would result in large companies with extensive catalogues of product and steady revenue streams. The existence of such a distribution infrastructure would permit European producers to 'plan and budget their productions from an early stage with transnational markets in mind affording them a viable means of raising their ambitions beyond merely national markets' (Media Business School, 1995: 4). Such gains would seem to require both distributor consolidation and vertical integration of the production and distribution levels. These larger integrated European producers would be able to carry a larger production slate to balance winners and losers as well as avoiding the necessity of giving up the rights to various territories and exhibition windows to raise production financing. Polygram, the only European distributor to operate across European territories, is already applying this approach (see Thomas, 1996: 504). It is also to be followed in the UK scheme to award franchises, in 1997, to be funded out of national lottery funding, to several consortia to develop, produce, and distribute films. But this is, of course, the much-maligned Hollywood model.

Such structural change would permit larger budgets both in development and in production. American film makers routinely invest up to 10 per cent of their budgets in development, while in Europe the proportion rarely exceeds one quarter of that figure. Production budgets in 1993 averaged $30 million for the majors and $9.4 for US independents, while the EU average was only $2.16 million. Even these low budgets were typically assembled only on the basis of government financial assistance from the many national and European Union programmes and co-production financing involving partners in two or more countries.

Probably the greatest difficulty facing the European film industry, however, is the traditional sharp cleavage between artistic and commercial goals. In Hollywood, creative decisions are made in a commercial context—what is expected to be of interest to a sizeable target audience. In Europe, directors have stoutly defended the importance of realizing their creative vision. Whether the audience is interested or not is sometimes a secondary consideration. The resulting tension between the business and creative forces has resulted in feature films that have been less appealing to audiences. On this point, Canadian culture critic Robert Fulford (1986: 8) asks:

Are there good Canadian movies on the shelves, callously ignored by U.S. distributors? . . . with rare exceptions, the films that are not distributed do not deserve distribution. The problem is with the producers who make so many bad films, rather than with the distributors; when good Canadian movies are made they usually get into theatres and find appropriate audiences.

The Japanese experience also suggests that US control of distribution is not the only factor. In fact distribution and exhibition are largely controlled by Toho and Shochiku, yet the US share of the Japanese box office is 55 per cent and rising.

## 5.7. WHAT CAN INDEPENDENT DISTRIBUTORS DO TO COMPETE WITH THE US MAJORS?

Feature films to be distributed are customarily categorized as either high-culture films conveying domestic cultural values or market-driven movies. The evidence on the distribution patterns of European films indicates that the films produced in each European nation have great difficulty in overcoming the cultural barriers faced as they cross national boundaries, even within Europe. But national distinctiveness may not be the cause of the problem. A recent study by Finn, Hoskins and McFadyen (1996) found no support for the proposition that identifiably Canadian movies were less commercially successful in the North American market (which is, of course, dominated by the US share of the total box office). This points to the high-culture nature of the product being the problem. Independent film-makers in Canada and Europe tend to target a different audience from that aimed at by the Hollywood majors. The majors direct their product to younger demographics, the key moviegoing audience, whereas independent film-makers in Canada and Europe have traditionally targeted a domestic audience of adults and a foreign audience of sophisticated filmgoers (again, mainly adults).

London Economics (1992) for instance, after noting that 'the dominance of the US majors, the special attraction for exhibitors of their particular pipeline of product, and their likely bias against EC product may well contribute to difficulties for independent EC producers in screening their products', observes: 'we are facing a classic chicken and egg problem: there is little point in organizing massive finance or distribution if we carry on making the films we do; but there is no point in trying to make large mass market films unless we organize better distribution and finance.'

So what is to be done? Maybe nothing. There are two distinct models for film distribution, and indeed the whole feature film business at hand—the Hollywood model and the independent production model. Both models have their advantages. European film-makers who wish to work on market-driven product directed at the young can do so within the Hollywood system, which is always on the lookout for talent wherever it is located in the world. This does not rule out action under competition law for any unlawful market conduct following from the market power of the majors.

Those with other goals should realize that the independent production model has advantages of its own.

It is easier to have one-off, or sporadic, successes in the art-house sector. The need for a single distributor to feed a pipeline of films is reduced. The need to have a coordinated release pattern is reduced, because audience discrimination is more sophisticated. There are a smaller number of theaters to be coordinated anyway. Moreover, the lower budget films are easier to organize than large budget films . . . The Europeans also have a strong advantage over LA in making films for their own domestic audiences on domestic themes. (London Economics, 1992: 66)

The importance of this last point should not be overlooked by those concerned about cultural objectives.

Finally, we should take note of the fact that, although this debate has developed over time in terms of the feature film industry, it is now becoming increasingly relevant to television distribution. Jeff Schlesinger, president of Warner Bros. International TV, warns us that the Americans are no longer willing to consign themselves to the role of content providers:

Two years ago , we were primarily in the distribution business, with no foreign-based channels, no investments abroad and no co-productions. Now we have a more efficient distribution system, we are setting up thematic channels around the world and we are undertaking clearly-defined local and co-production opportunities.

The media mega-mergers in the US have put the US majors in an even more dominant position. As Wilfred Ahrens observes:

Europeans will have no chance to catch up with the structural advantage the big media mergers have created for the Americans; the vertical integration of production and distribution plus the bandwidth of profit windows, the marketing of a film through a chain of money-making outlets: theater, pay-per-view, video (sales and rental), pay-TV, video discs, free TV, merchandising—all in one hand. (*Television Business International*, Mar. 1996, p. 20)

But rather than considering this a counsel of doom, if creativity and cultural goals are paramount, the opportunities remaining within this American-dominated system for independent producers around the world may be both artistically and commercially attractive.

# 6

# *Export Pricing of Television Programmes*

In this chapter we examine the pricing of television programmes on the international market. A widespread concern is the low level of US export prices. The low US export prices for programmes of high production quality make it extremely difficult for producers of drama based elsewhere to compete in their home market (let alone foreign markets). This, in turn, has led some observers to claim that US distributors are 'dumping' or selling US programmes below cost in export markets in a deliberate attempt to stifle the efforts of foreign competitors to introduce their own programming. For example, Schiller (1971: 101) has accused the United States of dumping in low-income areas of Africa and Asia.

Throughout the chapter, for convenience, pricing is discussed in terms of individual programmes, although programmes (especially feature films) are sometimes sold in packages or in output deals that give a broadcaster the rights to all of a studio's products. For example, RTL, the German broadcaster, spent 350 million marks in 1995 on a large film package from Time-Warner. Barter is also sometimes involved. For example, in the mid-1980s CBS and CCTV, of the People's Republic of China, reached an exchange agreement. CCTV were permitted to select sixty-four hours of programming from CBS total inventory and, in return, CBS was allocated advertising time to sell on CCTV (see Cryan et al., 1988: 17).

The chapter is organized as follows. First we identify the actual level of prices for exported programmes. Then we explain the determination of these prices. In general terms we examine the role of demand (revenue) and cost in pricing decisions. We then apply this analysis to the demand (revenue structure) and supply (cost structure) for television programming. Bringing demand and supply considerations together, we explain a typical US producer's investment and pricing decisions. Finally we address the issue of whether the pricing of US programme exports is 'unfair' and raise some policy implications.

## 6.1. PRICES AND THE GLOBAL MARKET FOR TV PROGRAMMING

Export prices per half-hour or hour of television programming are available from *Television Business International* (*TBI*), *Variety*, *Video Age*, and *TV World*. They differ somewhat in country coverage, programming categories, and historical availability. 1995 prices reported by *TBI Yearbook 95* (p. 282), given as a low–high range which depends on the type and quality of the programme, are shown in Table 6.1. Two features of the prices of television programmes in the global market stand out. First, there is no one export price for all foreign markets, but rather a different price for each market. Second, the export prices are usually much below production cost. We consider each of these characteristics in turn.

### 6.1.1. *Price discrimination*

Instead of a uniform international price applying throughout a worldwide market there are national markets with prices differing considerably: for example, the BBC or ITV in the UK pay \$20,000–\$100,000 per commercial hour (50 minutes), Germany \$15,000–\$80,000, Belgium \$3,000–\$5,000, Zimbabwe \$200–\$250, and Aruba (in the Caribbean) \$80–\$100. For some nations there are separate language markets. Thus in Canada the CBC English Network pays \$12,000–\$60,000 while the CBC French Network pays \$10,000–\$25,000. With the rise of cable and satellite channels the price will vary by the type of exhibitor. This is reflected in the prices shown for the US and UK in Table 6.1. In the US a programme sale to a main network is made for \$100,000–\$2,000,000 per hour, while one to a basic cable channel goes for \$10,000 –\$250,000. The market for television programmes, unlike that for commodities, is thus not perfectly competitive. If it were perfectly competitive, the price would be determined by the interaction of global supply and demand, buyers and sellers would be price-takers, and all buyers would pay the same price for a given programme. In fact, the price paid by broadcasters for, as an example, an episode of *ER* varies tremendously from buyer to buyer. In economic terminology the ability to sell units of the same product (produced and distributed for the same cost) in different markets for different prices is called price discrimination.

A number of conditions must be present for price discrimination to take place. First, it must be possible for the seller to separate markets and keep them separate. Otherwise all buyers will buy in the market with the lowest price. A broadcaster buys a licence to exhibit a programme in a prescribed geographical area for a given number of occasions during a certain period. In general sellers have been successful in keeping the markets for television programmes separate, although there is a problem with bootlegged copies

TABLE 6.1. World programme price guide, 1995 ($)

| | Lower | Higher |
|---|---|---|
| *North America* | | |
| Canada | | |
| CBC English | 12,000 | 60,000 |
| CBC French | 10,000 | 25,000 |
| CTV | 10,000 | 60,000 |
| US | | |
| Main network | 100,000 | 2 m |
| Pay cable | 50,000 | 1.25 m |
| Basic cable | 10,000 | 250,000 |
| PBS network | 35,000 | 100,000 |
| Syndication | 20,000 | 120,000 |
| | | |
| *Central and South America* | | |
| Argentina | 1,500 | 5,000 |
| Bolivia | 200 | 500 |
| Brazil | 2,500 | 12,000 |
| Chile | 1,000 | 6,000 |
| Colombia | 2,500 | 6,500 |
| Costa Rica | 500 | 1,500 |
| Cuba | 400 | 800 |
| Ecuador | 1,000 | 2,200 |
| El Salvador | 400 | 630 |
| Guatemala | 330 | 450 |
| Honduras | 200 | 430 |
| Mexico | 2,500 | 10,000 |
| | | |
| Spain | 8,000 | 30,000 |
| Sweden | 3,000 | 8,000 |
| Switzerland | 2,500 | 5,000 |
| Turkey | 1,500 | 3,000 |
| UK | | |
| BBC/ITV | 20,000 | 100,000 |
| Channel 4 | 15,000 | 70,000 |
| Satellite | 2,000 | 70,000 |
| Cable | 2,000 | 4,000 |
| | | |
| *Eastern Europe* | | |
| Albania | 200 | 300 |
| Bulgaria | 500 | 800 |
| Czechoslovakia | 600 | 2,000 |
| Hungary | 800 | 1,000 |
| Poland | 750 | 1,500 |
| Romania | 700 | 1,000 |
| CIS | 800 | 4,000 |
| Ex-Yugoslavia | 800 | 1,500 |
| | | |
| *Asia and the Far East* | | |
| Bangladesh | 200 | 400 |
| Brunei | 250 | 500 |
| China | 1,000 | 2,000 |
| Hong Kong | 1,500 | 4,000 |
| | | |
| Dubai | 600 | 875 |
| Iran | 750 | 1,500 |
| Iraq[b] | 800 | 1,000 |
| Israel | 800 | 2,200 |
| Jordan | 600 | 800 |
| Kuwait | 1,000 | 1,200 |
| Lebanon | 300 | 500 |
| Malta | 100 | 300 |
| Qatar | 600 | 875 |
| Saudi Arabia | 1,500 | 2,000 |
| Syria | 400 | 650 |
| Yemen (North or South) | 500 | 1,500 |
| | | |
| *Africa* | | |
| Algeria | 250 | 750 |
| Angola | 200 | 600 |
| Bophuthatswana | 500 | 700 |
| Egypt | 1,000 | 1,200 |
| Ethiopia | 200 | 600 |
| Gabon | 200 | 750 |
| Kenya | 250 | 750 |
| Mauritius | 175 | 200 |
| Morocco | 400 | 650 |

|  |  |  |
|---|---|---|
| Nicaragua | 140 | 350 |
| Panama | 300 | 800 |
| Paraguay | 140 | 500 |
| Peru | 700 | 1,200 |
| Uruguay | 300 | 660 |
| Venezuela | 2,000 | 7,000 |
| *Western Europe* | | |
| Austria | 3,500 | 8,000 |
| Belgium | 3,000 | 5,000 |
| Denmark | 2,500 | 5,000 |
| Finland | 2,500 | 5,500 |
| France | 8,000 | 60,000 |
| Germany | 15,000 | 80,000 |
| Gibraltar | 200 | 200 |
| Greece | 2,000 | 4,000 |
| Iceland | 800 | 1,000 |
| Ireland | 1,500 | 2,000 |
| Italy | 10,000 | 55,000 |
| Luxembourg | 1,300 | 4,000 |
| Netherlands | 4,000 | 9,000 |
| Norway | 1,500 | 5,000 |
| Portugal | 2,500 | 4,000 |
| India | 1,000 | 2,000 |
| Indonesia | 700 | 1,500 |
| Japan | | |
| NHK | 20,000 | 50,000 |
| Commercial | 25,000 | 120,000 |
| South Korea | 750 | 1,500 |
| Macau | 1,400 | 1,700 |
| Malaysia[a] | 1,000 | 2,000 |
| Pakistan | 600 | 1,000 |
| Philippines | 1,000 | 1,700 |
| Singapore | 700 | 1,000 |
| Sri Lanka | 300 | 500 |
| Taiwan | 600 | 750 |
| Thailand | 600 | 1,500 |
| *Oceania* | | |
| Australia | | |
| ABC | 2,000 | 4,000 |
| Commercial | 11,000 | 45,000 |
| New Zealand | 20,000 | 100,000 |
| Abu Dhabi | 1,500 | 6,000 |
| Bahrain | 500 | 875 |
| Cyprus | 500 | 650 |
| Namibia | 400 | 500 |
| Nigeria | 1,500 | 3,000 |
| Seychelles | 125 | 200 |
| South Africa | 3,500 | 8,500 |
| Swaziland | 100 | 200 |
| Tunisia | 500 | 700 |
| Zambia | 200 | 300 |
| Zimbabwe | 200 | 250 |
| *Caribbean* | | |
| Aruba | 80 | 100 |
| Bahamas | 200 | 250 |
| Barbados | 200 | 250 |
| Bermuda | 100 | 200 |
| Cuba | 400 | 450 |
| Dominican Republic | 200 | 600 |
| Haiti | 100 | 200 |
| Jamaica | 100 | 200 |
| Netherlands Antilles | 100 | 200 |
| Puerto Rico | 1,500 | 7,000 |
| St Maarten | 100 | 120 |
| Trinidad and Tobago | 300 | 400 |

[a] If telecast prior to Singapore.
[b] Prices which could be commanded during normal times.

*Source: Television Business International Yearbook 95* (London: Media and Telecoms), p. 282.

in certain parts of the world (this is more of a factor for feature films and video).

Second, sellers have to enjoy an element of market power which permits them to be price-setters rather than being forced to accept a uniform price determined by the impersonal forces of supply and demand. Some degree of market power is provided by product differentiation, as each programme is different. In addition, historically there is some evidence of collusion among US exporters. Guback (1984: 160) states that the history of the feature film and television programming distribution industry 'reveals a proclivity for collusion, parallel behavior to restrain trade, and anti competitive practices'. According to Renaud and Litman (1985: 247), 'operations of many [US] distribution companies overseas follow an oligopolistic pattern that led early to price-setting'. Competition from non-US producers provides a constraint on price-setting. However, US producers act like a dominant firm and are responsible for the general level of foreign programme prices in most markets, while producers in other countries take the US price as given and price their own product accordingly.

Third, price discrimination can only be a profitable strategy if the price elasticity of demand differs between markets. Price elasticity of demand is a measure of responsiveness of quantity demanded to changes in price, and is calculated as the percentage change in quantity demanded/percentage change in price. It can be viewed as an indicator of willingness to pay. Suppose the same 10 per cent increase in price of a programme would result in a decrease in sales of 30 per cent in Market A (an elasticity of 3 as the decrease in quantity demanded is threefold the increase in price) but only 5 per cent (elasticity of 0.5) in Market B. Such a price increase will lead to a substantial decrease in revenue in Market A (and only be profitable if the reduction in cost from needing to supply a smaller volume is even greater) but an increase in revenue (and hence profits) in Market B. Notice that the revenue goes up in Market B as a result of the price having risen 10 per cent with only a 5 per cent drop in quantity demanded. To be classified as price discrimination, the differences in prices observed must be a reflection of differences in demand conditions rather than reflections of differences in cost of supplying. We will explore the determinants of demand later in this chapter.

### 6.1.2. *The low level of export prices*

An inspection of Table 6.1 indicates another feature of prices of television exports: their low level relative to production cost. Excepting the US itself, the highest price is the $120,000 a Japanese commercial channel may pay, but even this is only about 10 per cent of the likely production cost for such a programme. The production cost is roughly twelve times the $100,000 high-end price BBC or ITV in the UK would expect to pay, twenty times the $60,000 paid by a broadcaster in France, and 12,000 times the $100 price paid by Aruba. A key aspect of the success of US programme exports is the low level of prices charged.


## 6.2. DEMAND AND WILLINGNESS TO PAY

A seller with market power will aim to set the programme price at the reservation price, the economic term for the maximum price the broadcaster, speciality channel, or pay-channel is willing to pay. If the importer is a private broadcaster, the value of a programme to the broadcaster depends on the value of the programme to advertisers. This will be a function of the number of viewers expected and the worth of each viewer. The number of viewers will depend primarily on the market size (potential audience) and share of this market expected. The share, in turn, will depend on the degree of competition from other channels and the extent of the cultural discount. If the programme is 'alien', then the cultural discount will be large and a smaller proportion of the potential audience will be attracted. The worth of each viewer to the advertiser is mainly related to viewer income.

These determinants of value to a private broadcaster should also apply to a public broadcaster. Increasingly, public broadcasters rely partially on advertising revenue. Even where this is not the case, such as for the BBC in the UK, there is pressure to compete in audience ratings in order to maintain a significant market presence that can be used to justify a continuing public subsidy or licence fee. In any case, most public broadcasters compete with private broadcasters to purchase popular US programming, and hence have to pay the commercially determined going rate.

For a pay-per-view channel the value of a programme will be directly determined by the expected revenue it will earn.


## 6.3. COST AND WILLINGNESS TO SUPPLY TELEVISION PROGRAMMES

As we saw in Chapter 3, television programming is a joint-consumption product and hence the incremental cost of supplying a programme to an additional export market is very low. It follows that it is profitable, in the sense that the revenue from the sale exceeds the out-of-pocket cost, to export at low prices.

A buyer with market power, just like a seller with market power, will have its own view of the optimal price. Such a buyer would like to pay the minimum price at which the seller would be willing to supply, namely the incremental cost of supplying. Buyer market power may exist because there is only a single broadcast purchaser. Until relatively recently, many countries had only their public broadcaster. For instance in Europe, even as late as 1981, only the UK and Italy had private broadcasters.

Buyer power can also result from collusion between potential purchasers. The UK provides an example. Historically, the ITV companies did not usually purchase foreign programmes directly but acted through ITV's Film Purchase Group. Furthermore, there was 'an understanding' between BBC and ITV not to compete for the same series. However, on occasion such buyer collusion broke down. For example, in 1985 World Vision wanted to raise the price of *Dallas* from £29,000 to £54,000 per episode. The BBC, which had shown *Dallas* since 1979, was still fighting this when Thames TV quite separately agreed to buy the programmes at the asked-for price. Thames's move was unorthodox because it bypassed the central ITV purchasing system (Schlesinger, 1986: 282).

International purchasing collusion also occurs. The European Broadcasting Union (EBU) acts as 'the sole negotiator on behalf of its member countries for the rights to international events, and controls programme distribution between member organizations' (Noam, 1993: 45). This has kept down the price paid for events such as the Olympic Games and soccer's World Cup.

However, market power on the buying side is becoming increasingly difficult to maintain given the explosion of off-air, cable, and satellite channels, all of which are competing for attractive programming.

## 6.4. DEMAND AND SUPPLY: THE INVESTMENT AND PRICING DECISIONS

In this section, based on Hoskins, Mirus and Rozeboom (1989), we first consider the investment decision of the producer who is considering whether to go ahead with the programme. We then examine the pricing decision.

### 6.4.1. *The investment decision*

An explanation of the export pricing of programming begins with the sales opportunities presented when a television series or film is first produced. For illustrative purposes we will examine this issue with respect to a producer from the US, the dominant exporting country, and assume that the programme is a drama series. However, although the details will vary, what we will say largely applies to a producer domiciled in any other country.

A licence to exhibit the series can be sold to a US network and to broadcasters in foreign markets for a first run (usually two showings). Initial screening rights can be sold to only one broadcaster in each market, as to do otherwise would reduce the value of the series to each purchaser and presumably result in less revenue in the aggregate. However, as we have noted, the market does not necessarily consist of an entire country. If the first run is successful and sufficient episodes get made, subsequent sales to the syndication market become possible later. Syndication typically involves sales to individual stations which run the programme five days a week in a non-prime time slot, such as 5 p.m. to 6 p.m.

Most of the costs quoted for producing a drama series, about $1.2 million or so per hour episode, are incurred in shooting the 'first copy'. Such figures are not solely incremental: they will include studio overhead allocations of up to 30 per cent. The costs of making another copy of an episode for a foreign market or syndication are very small in comparison. Such costs may include the cost of another physical copy of the film or tape, residuals paid to artists, dubbing/subtitling (if borne by the exporter rather than the importer), marketing and distribution costs, and, for tapes, possibly the cost of conversion from NTSC to PAL or SECAM standard.

From the producer's perspective, the decision to shoot a television series can be viewed as an investment decision. Investments involve spending money up-front in the hope of earning net revenues later. If the Internal Rate of Return (IRR), the return generated by the investment, is greater than the interest rate or cost of raising funds, then the investment should go ahead, as the producer will earn a surplus or profit. In terms of a television series, the net revenues are made up of the sum of the price minus attributable cost for each sales opportunity. The up-front costs are the original production cost. All revenues and costs should be assessed on an after-tax basis. Mathematically the IRR is $r$, which solves:

$$B_1 / (1 + r) + B_2 / (1 + r)^2 \dots B_n / (1 + r)^n = C,$$

where B is the net revenue and the subscript denotes the year the net revenue is received, C is the initial production cost, and $n$ is the number of years for which sales are made.

For illustrative purposes let us look back at the example we used in Chapter 4. We assumed that a US documentary costing $200,000 to produce resulted in revenues of $218,000. However, normally the net revenue is received after the production cost has been incurred. If we assume that all the net revenue is received one year after the production cost has been incurred, and there are no tax implications, the IRR is $r$ which solves: $218,000/(1 + r) = 200,000$. In this example, the IRR is 9 per cent. As long as this is an acceptable rate of return, which it will be if funds can be obtained for less than this, the producer will invest in production of the programme.

After looking over the story idea (conveyed in a short 'treatment'), but before funding the script, the networks and programme producers sign a 'pilot and series' contract which not only stipulates what share of the costs the network will pay for the pilot but also gives the network the renewal option at a set fee for each year up through the fifth year or longer.

The US network licence fee for a first-run programme typically pays 70–85 per cent of a programme's costs (although, when we consider that these costs include an overhead allocation that is not affected by whether the series goes ahead, most of the incremental costs of the series may be covered). Estimates can be made of probable sales to foreign markets and the prices in these markets. Given the low level of export prices, many foreign sales are necessary in order for net revenue from this source to be substantial. However, the trade literature suggests that the expected level of foreign sales is increasingly becoming a factor taken into account in the decision whether to produce. *Baywatch* is an example of a programme where the revenue from foreign sales was sufficient to justify the cost of additional episodes even after the series had been cancelled by a US network.

Most uncertain are the net revenues from syndication. Historically at least sixty-five episodes were regarded as necessary for syndication (five per week for thirteen weeks), although the number has fallen recently. This number of episodes will be available only if the US network renews the series for several seasons. If this does not occur, syndication will bring in zero net revenue; if it does occur, syndication can be very lucrative. For example, Turner Entertainment Group has obtained the rights to 88 episodes of *ER* (for rerun on its cable channel) from Warner Bros. for $105.6 million or $1.2 million per episode—the highest such price ever recorded (*Globe and Mail*, ' "ER" reruns net $1.2 million', 30 Jan. 1996, p. A6).

The key to whether a series goes ahead is a first-run commitment. This commitment will be based on audience reaction to a pilot and network assessment of the value to an advertiser of the demographic characteristics of the audience likely to be attracted. If a commitment is made, then the series is profitable for the producer on an expected IRR basis. The incremental costs of the series are met by the US network and foreign sales revenue, and there is the possibility of lucrative syndication revenues. Because the US network looms so large in this equation, its decision to license a programme for first run triggers the producer's 'go-ahead' investment decision.

At any one time, and over time, the larger producers will in effect have a portfolio of series accepted by the networks. Although money may be lost on some series that are cancelled early by the networks, any such losses will be more than offset by huge profits on the occasionally highly successful show such as *M\*A\*S\*H*, *Dallas*, *Seinfeld*, or *ER*. Of course, an individual series can be profitable even though none of the markets (first-run US network, US syndication, or foreign sales) may alone provide revenues that cover the production cost.

### 6.4.2. *The pricing decision*

Once the investment decision to make a programme has been made and the production cost sunk, the producer next needs to determine how many foreign markets to supply (and hence how many copies of the programme episode should be made) and at what prices. These issues are examined in Fig. 6.1.

Addressing the second question first, the US producer would like to sell to a broadcaster/distributor in each country, including its own domestic market, at the reservation price, the maximum price a broadcaster or distributor would be willing to pay. However, as we have seen, a broadcaster will have its own view of what the optimal price is. The broadcaster would like to pay the minimum price a producer would be willing to supply for. This minimum price is equal to the incremental cost of making and distributing a copy of the programme. Economists call this additional cost of supplying one more unit the 'marginal cost'. In Fig. 6.1 marginal cost (MC) is shown as constant. However, it may be reduced for some adjacent markets if the same copy is 'bicycled' from market to market—this is commonly done for parts of the Caribbean.

The actual price will usually be determined through negotiation and will lie between the reservation price and the marginal cost. The final price

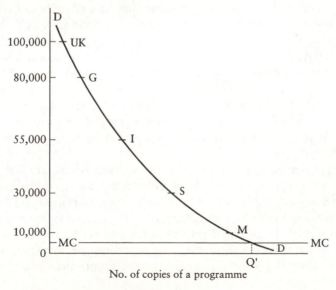

No. of copies of a programme

FIG. 6.1. Programme prices in export markets

agreed on will depend on the market power and bargaining skill of the parties. Market power depends on the options available. What alternative broadcasters could the producer sell to in the given market? What alternative suppliers are available to the broadcaster? Some examples can illustrate the effect of changes in the degree of market power on the buyer side on the price paid for US programming. One instance, already cited, is the almost doubling of the price of *Dallas* to the UK when competition broke out amongst buyers. In Canada, prices rose by 40 per cent after the entry of Global in 1974 introduced buyer competition. In Australia, prices approximately doubled in the late 1980s following the breakup of the major networks' cooperative arrangements for buying programmes (BTCE, 1991). In Italy, when extensive deregulation increased buyer competition, maximum programme prices (as reported by *Variety*) increased by more than 1,000 per cent between 1981 and 1985.

Starting with the price in its domestic market and then ranking export markets by descending order of actual prices traces out the demand curve D in Fig. 6.1. The demand curve shows the number of units that can be sold at different prices. Using the high end of the price ranges in Table 6.1, points on this demand curve would include, for example, a sale to the UK at $100,000, Germany (location on the demand curve shown as G) at $80,000, Italy (I) at $55,000, Spain (S) at $30,000, and Mexico (M) at $10,000.

With respect to the number of copies of a programme to supply, the US producer will supply another copy for sale to an additional foreign market if the price that can be agreed upon is greater than the marginal cost of supplying. This follows because, as each copy is sold independently to a different broadcaster in a different country at a different price, the incremental revenue received by the producer from a given sale is equal to the price paid. Hence any price above marginal cost will contribute toward sunk production costs. In Figure 6.1, Q' markets will be supplied up to where the marginal cost curve (MC) cuts the demand curve (D). If marginal cost is less than $100 it will be worth selling to Aruba, if the marginal cost is more it will not be. The mere fact that a price of $100 has been established for Aruba indicates that some producers, at least, have marginal costs below this.

The major elements of our theoretical analysis thus indicate that US producers of TV programmes are the dominant supplier in the international market and act as price-setters, that the variation in prices paid by different countries for a copy of a programme is the result of differences in willingness to pay, and that the degree of buyer competition in a market will influence the actual price negotiated (anywhere in the range from the reservation price that the seller would like to the supply price that the buyer would like).

### 6.4.3. Empirical evidence

A study by Hoskins, Mirus, and Rozeboom (1989) provides empirical support for the model of US export price determination described above. The statistical method used was multiple regression, which isolates the individual effect of each variable while holding all others constant. As expected, they found price positively related to the size (number of TV sets) and wealth (per capita GNP) of the importing market. Markets with a single broadcaster paid about 55 per cent less than markets with competing broadcasters. English-language markets, presumably because of a lower cultural discount, paid higher prices than other language markets for US programmes. These four variables were able to explain about 70 per cent of the observed price variations.

## 6.5. THE LOW LEVEL OF EXPORT PRICES: UNFAIR PRICING?

The low level of US export prices have led to allegations of dumping. Dumping is usually defined as occurring if either of the following conditions apply:

1. The price charged in the foreign market is below cost.
2. The price the producer charges in the foreign market is less than the producer charges for the same product in its own domestic market.

Taken at face value, both of these conditions would appear to be met.

However, when it is said that US export prices are 'low' and below cost, the reference-point is the 'high' production cost in the United States or the 'high' cost to the foreign producer (often the broadcaster) of producing an indigenous substitute. But our analysis indicates that a comparison to production cost is not appropriate because this cost is not attributable to a sale to an additional export market. The relevant cost is the low marginal cost of making an additional copy (and even this is not always necessary) and distributing it to that export market. In major markets at least, the price paid is far in excess of this incremental cost of supplying the market.

With respect to the second condition, at least for a programme sold to a US network, the foreign prices are invariably below the domestic price. This is because the US market is uniquely large and wealthy and because there is a cultural discount applied to US programming in foreign markets but not in the US domestic market.

But the prices in Table 6.1 relate to exports from all sources and not just the US. Thus non-US exporters also sell at low prices, in fact often below the US price for a similar programme because they lack the US 'brand

name'. For example, Marques de Melo (1995) reports that Brazilian telenovelas are priced for export at around one-third the level of US series. Thus
non-US exporters also sell at a price below production cost. Also, every
non-US exporter sells programmes in at least some foreign markets for less
than the price charged in the domestic market. For non-US producers, the
presence of a cultural discount for exports would lead us to expect a price
below the domestic one in at least all foreign markets with an equal or
smaller market size.

In summary, the charge of dumping is virtually meaningless for a joint-
consumption good. If the US is guilty, so is every other exporting country.
For example, if France sells a programme to a Belgian broadcaster, it does
so at a price which is below production cost. If an independent producer
in the UK sells a programme to ABC in Australia, it does so at a lower price
than it charges the BBC.

## 6.6. THE POLICY IMPLICATIONS

Our analysis emphasizes that it is an unusual economic characteristic of
television programming, namely the joint-consumption property, that
explains the low export price. Most of the cost is associated with developing and producing the original film or tape of the programme, which can
then be copied and distributed to additional markets at minimal incremental cost. This does not provide comfort to foreign producers or policy-
makers because it means that they cannot justifiably accuse the US of
dumping.

However, it is these low prices which have abetted the penetration of US
programming and, in part, led to allegations of cultural imperialism. It is
the low export prices, for programmes of high production quality, that
make it difficult for drama producers in other countries to compete against
US programmes in their domestic market, let alone foreign markets. For
example, a broadcaster in Canada can acquire rights to a US drama series
for about one-tenth of the cost of producing in-house or one-quarter the
cost of acquiring a series from a Canadian independent producer. In most
markets, because of the cultural discount, the more expensive of the domestic dramas tend to outdraw the US series and attract more advertising
revenue, but this revenue advantage must be substantial in order to out-
weigh the cost disadvantage. Sometimes it is. For example, in India, Star
Television has found that, since low Indian production costs limit the cost
disadvantage, the much greater popularity of domestic programming can
make it economically viable.

# 7

# The Rationale for Government Intervention, and Implications for Assessing Trade Disputes

In this chapter we first examine the reasons given for government intervention. We are then in a position to evaluate appropriate public policies and assess the trade disputes, described in Chapter 1 (section 1.3), concerning the legitimacy of protection and subsidy of television and film. The rationales we consider have been identified by Graham and Davies (1992), Peacock (1986), Brown (1996),Throsby (1994), Hoskins and McFadyen (1985; 1992) and others. Often the arguments have been couched in terms of support for public service broadcasting, but they have broader applicability. We consider them in terms of television and film production, distribution, and exhibition.

## 7.1. RATIONALE FOR GOVERNMENT INTERVENTION

### 7.1.1. *External benefits*

In economic terminology, an externality is a cost or a benefit arising from an economic transaction which falls on a third party and is not taken into account by either party to the transaction. External costs in the form of pollution and associated environmental problems are quite common and well recognized, but external benefits are less so. Education is an example of a good that is commonly agreed to provide external benefits.

For a given television programme or film to be judged as providing an external benefit, viewing by one person must generate benefits to other members of society through improved social interaction. The crucial question is thus whether the content of audiovisual products affects social behaviour. While the academic literature on this is somewhat inconclusive, the ongoing debate with respect to violent television programmes, films, and videos indicates a common belief that audiovisual content is influential. But if 'bad' content can have undesirable effects on society (i.e. impose an external cost) it is reasonable to suppose that 'good' content can have desirable effects. For example, indigenous drama programming or feature films may provide external benefits in the form of an increased sense of national identity, and awareness of community themes and values. In the context of feature films, André Guérin (president of Quebec's Régie du Cinéma et de la Vidéo) states:

A given population should from time to time be able to see itself on the screen. That just seems fundamental and not even for nationalistic reasons but because of questions of identity. Having constantly to deal with foreign models, you end up rather deeply damaged by the never-ending exposure to foreign dramatic situations.

Current affairs, news programming, and documentary programmes or films may promote a population more informed on national institutions, events, and issues and a home-grown perspective on foreign affairs. In Australia, an object of regulation of commercial television is 'to promote the role of broadcasting services in developing and reflecting a sense of Australian identity, character and cultural diversity' (Broadcasting Services Act, 1992, section 83). In effect, external benefits can be thought of as valuable side-effects resulting from viewing.

The concept of external benefits provides a bridge between the economic and cultural development approaches to public policy relating to audiovisual industries. The belief that indigenous programming and film possessing desirable attributes can make viewers better citizens is at the heart of both the external benefits and the 'cultural' argument. This is not widely appreciated; indeed the social importance of television and film in promoting citizenship is often listed as a non-economic justification for intervention. For example, Graham and Davies (1992) discuss external benefits under the heading 'Market Failure in Consumption' but under a separate heading, 'Citizenship, Culture and Community', continue to make an argument that, to our mind, is essentially a restatement of the external benefits rationale. Their argument, in the context of support for public broadcasting, is made particularly persuasively:

For the great majority of people (TV) is their major source of information about the world, beyond that of family, friends and acquaintances . . . [it is] also part of how we understand the community—indeed part of where the very idea of community arises and is given meaning . . . culture and community provide a common frame of reference in terms of which to comprehend the history, present and future of one's society and of one's own place within it, and so to make sense of the decisions one has to take both as an individual and as a citizen. (pp. 181–2)

In similar vein, the Mandate Review Committee (1996) in Canada states: 'We need Canadian programs . . . to enable our citizens to understand one another, to develop a national and community consciousness, to help us shape our own solutions to social and political problems, and to inspire the imagination of our children and express their hopes' (p. 31). They quote approvingly from Raboy et al. (1994: 38) who define cultural development as 'the process by which human beings acquire the individual and collective resources necessary to participate in public life'. The Mandate Review Committee conclude: 'With this in mind, Canadian programming on the CBC should be intended, first of all, for the active participation of Canadian citizens in the affairs of their country' (p. 43). However, like Collins (1990), we are dubious of some of the nation-building claims made for television programming, particularly drama. Collins argues that, to the contrary, 'Canada better represents a weak rather than a strong connection between television consumption and political identity and citizenship' (1990: 234).

If television programmes or films do provide external benefits, there is market failure because programme and film producers, distributors, and exhibitors do not receive any compensation from the market for the provision of such external consumption benefits. Government intervention is thus justified to the extent it compensates for this failure.

### 7.1.2. Inadequate programme diversity

This argument is that a limited number of competing private stations will offer excessive duplication of mass appeal programme types. This is based on the spatial competition model of Steiner (1952) predicting that an oligopoly (an industry with a few dominant firms) of private, advertising-financed broadcasters will offer few distinctive programme options, as each gets a higher rating from sharing the large audience for popular programming than from gaining all the audience for a minority-interest programme. Under such circumstances, funding of a public service broadcaster (or other form of intervention to ensure availability of minority programming) can better reflect consumer preferences. As Peacock (1986) explains, 'as long as the number of television channels is limited, and there is no direct consumer payment, collective provision and regulation of programmes does provide a better simulation of a market designed to reflect consumer preferences than a policy of *laissez-faire*'.

The example given in Table 7.1, based on Hoskins and Mirus (1988), illustrates this preference problem with ten viewers, A–J, and ten pro-

TABLE 7.1. Viewers' programme preferences

| Programme preference | Viewers | | | | | | | | | |
|---|---|---|---|---|---|---|---|---|---|---|
| | A | B | C | D | E | F | G | H | I | J |
| First | 10 | 7 | 4 | 10 | 7 | 4 | 10 | 7 | 4 | 2 |
| Second | 9 | 8 | 3 | 9 | 6 | 5 | 2 | 6 | 3 | 5 |
| Third | 1 | 1 | 1 | 1 | 1 | 1 | 1 | 1 | 1 | 1 |

*Source*: Hoskins and Mirus (1988: 507).

grammes, 1–10. The assumption is that people are prepared to watch television as long as they get at least their third preference. Thirty per cent of viewers rank programme 10 highest, 30 per cent programme 7 highest, and 30 per cent programme 4 highest. Nevertheless, if there were only three competing, advertising-financed, private broadcasters, none of these programmes would be shown. The reason is that each channel maximizes its audience (a 33 per cent share assuming the audience is equally split), and hence its advertising revenue, by showing programme 1. This is despite the fact that programme 1 is neither the first nor second choice of any of the viewers. It is the common denominator.

While not disputing the historical validity of this argument, we believe that technological developments, which are eliminating spectrum scarcity and permitting pay-per-view, are rapidly overcoming impediments to effective competition. In our example, adding a fourth channel would change the situation dramatically. Now programmes 10, 7, and 4 would each be offered. The reason is that the prospect of a 30 per cent share from offering programme 10, 7, or 4 (even though two channels would end up duplicating one of these programmes and only getting a 15 per cent share) is preferable to the 25 per cent share available if all channels exhibit programme 1.

A drawback of advertising financing is that the strength of viewers' preferences is not relevant. In the example above, three pay-per-view channels would probably provide programmes 10, 7, and 4 respectively. This is because the pay-per-view channels would be able to charge a higher price for a first-preference programme than for a third-preference programme. Hence a first-preference programme with a 30 per cent share would, in all probability, bring in more revenue than a third-preference programme with a 33 per cent share.

### 7.1.3. Merit goods

According to this rationale, certain programmes or films are 'meritorious' and should be made available even though individual demand is insufficient to induce supply. The government should adopt a paternalistic role by intervening in markets and substituting its own preferences for those expressed by individual consumers. Various reasons have been promoted for regarding goods as 'merit' goods worthy of public funding:

(a) The contention that the welfare of viewers is enhanced by the provision of certain programmes that would not be supplied by a market system. Viewing of such programmes makes them 'better people'.

(b) Current programme preferences reflect past availability. Consumption of good programmes and films is addictive in the sense that consumption today increases knowledge and appreciation and thus changes tastes in favour of future consumption. Such goods may eventually become economically viable after viewers have been exposed to them for some time.

(c) Some people will accept guidance or stimulus from others on matters where they perceive that their knowledge or taste is limited.

(d) Many people would like high-quality material to be available even though they would not willingly watch it themselves in large enough numbers for it to be paid for directly.

(e) Minority-interest programming directed at limited ethnic, intellectual, social, or cultural groups should be available.

We consider that the 'merit' argument is open to abuse because it provides a justification, often couched in vague terms, for governments or cultural elites to impose their own preferences. Reason (c) is a case in point.

Some of the reasons are no longer persuasive in a multi-channel environment. Where such an environment encompasses pay-per-view, the market itself, without intervention, can be expected to provide niche programming targeted at minority interests (see reason (e)). While (b) is undoubtedly true, in a multi-channel environment it is questionable whether many will choose to view such programmes or films sufficiently to acquire an appreciation.

Reasons (a) and (d) remain valid, but appear to be consistent with the external benefits rationale and can be subsumed under that category.

### 7.1.4. *Infant industry*

The infant industry argument is that a new domestic industry deserves protection and/or subsidy while it is young and vulnerable. Only if it is given this assistance will it achieve the size and maturity that enables it to compete in the international market. Size and maturity are important if there are substantial economies of scale and/or experience (learning).

If there are economies of scale, increased size is more efficient, as a given percentage increase in inputs results in a larger percentage increase in output per period, and hence average cost decreases. As we have seen earlier, the joint-consumption characteristic of television programmes and films does indeed lead to decreasing average cost as the audience increases. Maturity is relevant if the industry enjoys learning or experience economies. This concept suggests that, for complex goods, the average cost goes down as time and cumulative output increase because people learn through experience and adapt by making incremental improvements to the production process. This would seem to be the case for television and film production.

However, the essence of the infant industry argument is that the protection should be temporary, and withdrawn once the industry has matured.

The television and film industries in most developed countries can no longer be classified as infant industries, and hence intervention can no longer be supported on these grounds.

### 7.1.5. Economic development and employment

Justification for government support or protection is sometimes based on economic-development and employment-creating grounds. However, government support comes from taxes and it is not at all obvious that the expenditure by the government creates more jobs than are lost through the resulting reduction of expenditures and savings by those paying the taxes. Even if government investment in jobs is considered a viable approach, there remains the question whether an investment in television and film is more effective in this regard than the same investment in another sector.

### 7.2. RATIONALE FOR GOVERNMENT INTERVENTION: SUMMARY AND CONCLUSION

Several justifications have been put forward for government intervention to support television and film. The rationale we have always considered most persuasive (see e.g. Hoskins and McFadyen, 1985; 1992) is that based on external benefits. These arise if there are benefits to society as a whole (as opposed to direct benefits to the viewer personally) resulting from citizens being exposed to (some types of) indigenous programming. Hence the private sector, in the absence of a subsidy, will produce less than an optimal quantity of such programming. Government intervention is justified to the extent it compensates for these benefits.

However, there is still the possibility of ' "government failure"—that is, the cost of government action exceeding benefits' (Brown, 1996: 10). Some conclude that the economic case for subsidization of cultural products is not persuasive on the grounds that any benefits are likely to be outweighed by the costs (see e.g. Globerman, 1987).

In this context, it should be borne in mind that a prime strategy for firms in regulated industries is to lobby in order to make the regulatory rules, or their application, more industry-friendly. The argument used by industry groups will usually be couched in cultural-development terms even though the motive may be economic self-interest. The lobbying effort will often be coordinated by or channelled through industry associations. The Report of the Task Force on Broadcasting Policy, undertaken for the Canadian government, expressed surprise at private broadcasters' 'almost eager acceptance of regulations of some kind' (Canada, 1986). In fact, studies of the effects of cultural regulation by, for example, Globerman (1987), Janisch (1987), and Watson (1989) are consistent with the capture theory of regulation, first suggested by Stigler (1971). According to this theory, the regulator is captured by the industry and its regulations protect the interests of the existing firms in the regulated industry rather than the public, the latter being the assumption in the alternative public interest theory.

Thus, although we conclude that government intervention can legitimately be justified through the external benefits rationale, and do not consider that the costs of such support always exceed the benefits, we do believe that each case of intervention should be carefully assessed to see if it is consistent with the externalities argument and whether the benefits are commensurate with the cost.

### 7.3. TRADE DISPUTES: THE RELEVANCE OF EXTERNAL BENEFITS

As we noted in Chapter 1, trade in cultural goods has long been controversial, and came close to causing the collapse of the recent Uruguay round of GATT. Many countries, notably France and Canada, regard television programmes and film as essential to the preservation and promotion of distinctive values and hence the wellbeing of the nation-state. Policies such as imposition of quotas are thus supported on cultural development grounds. The US, on the other hand, considers the audiovisual industry as part of the entertainment industry, producing commercial products no different from any other. The US thus regards policies that hinder trade as simply protectionism. Cultural arguments are viewed as a convenient smokescreen for protection of national industries.

The concept of external benefits provides a framework for resolving this debate. The issue comes down to whether or not external benefits are associated with television programmes and films. Pure entertainment goods would not result in external benefits. Are television programming and film merely entertainment goods or do viewers generate benefits for others through social interaction? Earlier in this chapter we accepted the argument that some programming/film does result in external benefits. We thus believe that some government intervention can be justified. Our support for the position of countries such as France and Canada, however, is highly qualified. It is evident that many of the programmes/films supported or protected do not provide external benefits. Eligibility to qualify as domestic content for quota and subsidy schemes is invariably grounded on a points system which is based on the nationality of the inputs. However, the provision of external benefits can only be evaluated on the basis of the nature (or expected nature) of the final product. For example, *Night Heat*, produced by Alliance of Toronto, in the mid-1980s became the first foreign drama series to be picked up by a US network. In Canada this series qualified as Canadian content for quota purposes and received funding from

Telefilm Canada, the Canadian Government funding agency. However, the Canadian content of the programme was deliberately disguised in order to produce a generic North American product targeted at a US audience. Obviously there was no external benefit. Such a programme is merely an entertainment good, and support for programmes of this ilk does indeed amount to protection and as such distorts trade.

The dilemma is thus that, although external benefits provide a valid reason for public policies promoting programmes or films providing this property, it does not justify much of the government intervention that actually takes place. The US has reason to complain about many of the hindrances and distortions to trade. The difficulty is that trade rules tend to be all or nothing, and the disputants indeed seem to view the issue this way. Either national governments are free to impose quotas, provide subsidies, etc. as they see fit, or no such intervention can be permitted. Our analysis suggests that neither approach is optimal.

# 8

# *Public Policy: Support and Protection*

As we saw in Chapter 7, reasons given for government support and protection for television and film include external benefits, inadequate programme diversity, merit goods, infant industry, and economic development and employment arguments. In this chapter we examine the various forms—some being solely or largely applicable to television rather than film—that support and protection can take. These include:

funding a public broadcasting corporation or state film corporation;
direct subsidy to television programme or film production;
content regulations/quotas;
tax concessions;
entry barriers and licensing conditions;
international co-production treaties.

Most nations use a combination of these approaches. There are significant differences between nations in the mandate and funding of public broadcasters and the approaches used to subsidize production and protect the industry.

In this chapter we examine each of these forms of support. This examination includes an assessment of whether the method of support is consistent with the external benefits rationale which, as we have argued in Chapter 7, we consider a legitimate, though limited, justification for government intervention. Although we draw examples from a number of countries, we make no attempt to provide a nation-by-nation description of government policy in this area; this is beyond the scope of this book, and indeed could constitute a book in its own right.

## 8.1. PUBLIC BROADCAST (STATE FILM) CORPORATIONS

This section will focus on the role and funding of public broadcasting, as many nations have a public broadcaster whereas few have a state film corporation. To provide perspective, we first describe the worldwide crisis in public broadcasting, its causes, and its implications.

### 8.1.1. *The crisis in public broadcasting*

From the 1950s through to the early 1980s public broadcasting predomi-nated in most countries, and its role and level of funding were widely accepted. For example, in Western Europe only the UK and Italy had com-mercial television. However, this picture has changed radically, with com-mercial television coming to Germany in 1984; France and Iceland in 1986; Belgium in 1987; Denmark and Ireland in 1988; Spain in 1989; the Nether-lands, Greece, and Norway in 1990; and Portugal and Sweden in 1991. 'By the closing years of the 1980's . . . public broadcasting institutions and the notions of cultural and political discourse that undergird them seemed everywhere to be under serious attack' (Rowland and Tracey, 1990). Several changes in the broadcasting environment led to the worldwide crisis.

New distribution technologies have permitted an expansion of channel capacity. Capacity in a geographical market has increased from around four terrestrial signals in the 1950s to literally hundreds of channels, using digital compression technology in conjunction with fibre-optic cable or satellite, in the 1990s. During the last two decades, in many countries right-wing gov-ernments came to power. Typically these were averse to invasive regulation, favoured privatization, and were prepared to permit increases in channel capacity that the new technology made possible. The expansion in the number of channels that resulted has led to a decrease in the audience share of most public broadcasters (see Table 8.1 for examples). As audience share and audience totals decrease, people naturally begin to question the rele-vance of a public broadcaster and whether public funding, or the historic

TABLE 8.1. Declining audience share of public broad-casters (%)

|  | 1990 | 1992 | 1995 |
|---|---|---|---|
| BBC 1 (UK) | 38.1 | 33.6 | 31.4 |
| DR (Denmark) | 45.0 | 35.0 | |
| ET (Greece) | 19.6 | 10.5 | |
| SVT2/TV2 (Sweden) | 54.0 | 36.0 | |
| NRK (Norway) | 72.9 | 57.0 | |
| Nederland 1 (Netherlands) | 24.0 | 14.7 | |
| TVE 1 (Spain) | 53.6 | 32.6 | |
| RAI 1 (Italy) | 22.7 | 18.9 | |
| ARD (Germany) | 30.7 | 21.7 | |
| CBC (Canada) | 16.1 | | 12.9 |

*Source*: Except for Canada, *Screen Digest*, Oct. 1993 and Mar. 1995. For Canada, Mandate Review Com-mittee (1996).

level of public funding, can continue to be justified. This places the public broadcaster in a dilemma. If it competes aggressively for audience with 'common denominator' offerings it is accused of programming like a commercial broadcaster and hence of being redundant and unworthy of public funding, whereas if it provides distinctive, minority-taste programming its small audience brings into question its relevance and value for money (see e.g. Boardman and Vining, 1996; Blumler and Hoffman-Riem, 1992).

The increase in the number of channels undermines public broadcasting in another way. It leads to niche or speciality channels some of which may exhibit programming similar to that traditionally considered the prerogative of the public broadcaster. Examples include Arte, the Franco-German cultural channel, the History Channel in the US, and Bravo, which exhibits cultural (broadly defined) programming in Canada. Because they focus on a particular niche these channels may be seen as a better solution than the public broadcaster, which must try to continue to serve multiple niches. Another development is the poor financial status of many countries and the resulting preoccupation of governments with debts and deficits. In an era of government expenditure cutbacks, spending on public broadcasting is bound to come under close scrutiny.

### 8.1.2. *The role and programming of a public broadcaster*

What is the rationale for maintaining a public broadcaster in a multi-channel environment? While many of the traditional arguments for public funding no longer apply, we argued in Chapter 7 that one rationale, based on external benefits, remains persuasive. External benefits for broadcasting arise from benefits to society as a whole resulting from exposure to certain programming. Viewers of such programming become better citizens. There is then market failure because programme producers and exhibitors, whether advertising-financed or pay channels, do not receive revenue for the provision of such external benefits. Hence the private sector, in the absence of a subsidy, will produce less than an optimal quantity of such programming. Funding of a public broadcaster is one approach to rectifying the under-supply of programmes providing external benefits. The role of the public broadcaster should be to provide such programmes and, by so doing, complement the schedule of private broadcasters.

It would seem that some types of programming are more likely to provide external benefits than others. Current affairs, documentary, and news programming is likely to promote a population more informed on national events and issues, and a national perspective on foreign affairs. Drama programming may provide external benefits in the form of an increased sense of identity and awareness of national/regional themes and values. Children's programming can help educate and enlighten the young.

Complementary programming is likely to include cultural and minority-interest programming but also, as we have suggested, more general-interest programme types such as drama and documentaries. However, in such categories it is reasonable to expect differentiation from similar programmes offered by private broadcasters. There should be greater emphasis on domestic programming; as Blumler and Hoffman-Riem (1992: 30) observe, 'it falls on the public broadcaster to look to society's more indigenous needs'. In drama it is reasonable to expect a public broadcaster to be less concerned with 'jolts-per-minute'. For documentaries, news, and current affairs the public broadcaster should give more emphasis to analysis and less to sensationalism. More stress should be laid on innovation, risk-taking, and attempting to enlighten the audience.

The mandates of many public broadcasters have remained essentially unchanged as the industry structure has changed from a public-broadcast monopoly to a multi-channel environment where, in many countries, the public broadcaster is no longer a dominant player. It is no longer necessary for a public broadcaster to be all things to all people, and mandates should now reflect this. For example, some programme categories are best left to the private sector. Private broadcasters and special channels are only too happy to show professional sports, and it is difficult to justify the emphasis some public broadcasters continue to give to such programming. The only real beneficiaries are the sports themselves, as competition drives up the price of licensing rights. On a similar argument, US action drama can be left to the private sector.

Another issue is whether the programming exhibited by a public broadcaster should be produced in-house or purchased from independent producers. Traditionally many public broadcasters, such as the BBC in the UK and NHK in Japan, relied on in-house production for most of their domestic content. NHK still does, but the BBC is now required to procure at least 25 per cent of its non-news programming from independents. Continuing in-house production of programming with a short lead time, notably news and current affairs, certainly seems justified. The answer is less clear for programme types such as drama, children's programming, and documentaries. The Channel 4 example in the UK demonstrates that high-quality public-service-type programming is possible without in-house production. In addition, there is typically far more pressure on private producers to be efficient. However, a case can be made for some continuing in-house production in order to establish standards and provide competition for the independent producers.

### 8.1.3. *Sources of funding of public broadcasting*

The major sources of funding are a licence fee or parliamentary appropriations. This is sometimes augmented by commercial advertising/sponsorship or subscription. For example, a licence fee is the sole source of funding for the main services of public broadcasters in the UK, Denmark, Norway, and Japan. A parliamentary appropriation is the sole source for ABC in Australia. Advertising supplements one or other of these sources in Austria, Canada, Finland, Germany, Greece, Ireland, Italy, and the Netherlands.

### 8.1.3.1. *Licence fee*

A licence fee is the traditional method, pioneered in the UK with the BBC. The licence fee is normally annual, and takes the form of a given amount per television receiver owned or per television household. This is sometimes supported over a parliamentary appropriation on the grounds that it is an independent source of income; however, as it is the government that enforces the licence fee and determines the level permitted, there may not be significant advantages in this respect. Indeed, it was in the context of a licence fee that the Peacock Committee (1986: 138) wrote: 'it would indeed be astonishing if he who paid the piper did not occasionally hint at the tune; and it would be equally astonishing if the piper did not occasionally anticipate his paymaster's call'. A licence fee is likely to provide a relatively stable and predictable level of funding, although there may be occasional fluctuations such as the windfall experienced by the BBC when colour receivers (with a higher licence fee) rapidly replaced black and white.

The licence fee approach has its disadvantages. It is relatively costly to administer and difficult to enforce. Evasion in European countries is estimated to range from a low of 4 per cent of TV households in the Netherlands to 15 per cent in Norway (*Screen Digest*, May 1996, p. 120). The fee is not related to the household's level of viewing of the public broadcaster. Viewed as a form of tax it is regressive, as the amount paid does not increase in proportion to household income.

### 8.1.3.2. *Parliamentary appropriation*

An annual parliamentary appropriation is paid out of general taxation and is as progressive as the tax regime in the country. Administration and enforcement is relatively simple. One problem the public broadcaster faces is the yearly uncertainty about the level of appropriation and the difficulty this causes for long-term planning in an industry where the product—the programme—can have a gestation period of several years. However, private businesses in all sectors of the economy face similar difficulties.

With an annual parliamentary vote on the appropriation, the government is regularly reminded of the cost and, as this is money from general taxation, the alternative uses for these funds. It is no surprise, in an era of government cutbacks in response to debts and deficits, that McKinsey and Company, a consulting group, found in a 1993 survey that public broadcasters who relied on direct funding by government (rather than on a licence fee) had been particularly hard hit by budget reductions. This reliance on direct funding also militates against true independence from the government, although (as we indicated earlier) when compared to a licence fee this may be largely a matter of degree.

### 8.1.3.3. Advertising

Reliance on advertising provides an incentive to compete with private broadcasters for audience ratings. Pursuit of audience is not in itself undesirable for a public broadcaster. Indeed, external benefits can only accrue as a result of viewing, and, other things being equal, the more viewers the greater the aggregate external benefit. The danger, however, is that pursuit of audiences, in order to earn advertising revenue, leads to 'common denominator' programmes devoid of external benefits or event (usually sports) programmes that would otherwise be carried by a commercial channel. Where the latter is the case, even where the programme exhibits external benefits, no incremental benefits in aggregate are generated.

The Canadian case provides an interesting exemplar of how pursuit of advertising revenue can influence programming decisions. From the mid-1980s the real level of parliamentary appropriation to the CBC has declined. The CBC, which traditionally generates about 20 per cent of its budget from advertising (the rest coming from parliamentary appropriations), has become more aggressive in pursuit of advertising revenue. The Mandate Review Committee traced the consequences for programming, and found that the CBC English-Language Network 'has subtly reduced its emphasis on children's programming and more serious drama; produced or commissioned less high profile arts programming; and provided less money for local and regional programming' (1996: 71). Some children's after-school programming has been replaced by old US series. At the same time, sports has increased from 18 per cent of the prime-time (7–11 p.m.) schedule in 1985–6 to 25 per cent in 1993–4. Sports programming now accounts for an incredible 37 per cent of CBC TV's prime-time output.

### 8.1.3.4. Subscription

Subscription is another possible source. Currently its use by public broadcasters is largely as a supplementary source for secondary services. For example, NHK in Japan uses subscription for its high-definition satellite service while CBC in Canada uses it for its cable-delivered all-news services. However, the Peacock Committee (1986) in the UK recommended that subscription should eventually replace the licence fee for funding the BBC. A problem with this suggestion is that any significant price would decrease the number of viewers, which would reduce the external benefit generated.

If the subscription takes the form of pay-per-view this does open up the possibility of public funding subsidizing consumption of programmes deemed to promote external benefits. We elaborate on this in section 8.2.

### 8.1.3.5. Summary

There is no clear winner between a licence fee and a parliamentary appropriation. Subscription charges have a certain appeal, but restrict the external benefits generated. However, requiring or permitting a public broadcaster to raise advertising revenue is undesirable because it undermines provision of public-service programming.

## 8.2. DIRECT SUBSIDY TO TELEVISION PROGRAMME OR FILM PROVISION

Some countries provide generous direct funding to independent producers. Included in this group are France, Norway, Australia, and Canada. In countries with a federal government structure, such as Australia, Canada, and Germany, subsidies are often available from two levels of government. Countries such as Japan, the UK, and the US have overall been less generous, although some US states provide incentives through state film commissions, and federal tax credits were available from the early 1970s to mid-1980s (see Guback, 1985a). Also, beginning in 1997, some UK national lottery funding will be allocated to independent film production.

Where given, the subsidy is for production and, in some cases, project development, marketing, and even distribution. Government funding may come from general taxation, as in Australia and Canada, lottery funding, as in the UK, or a levy on items such as box office admission or television broadcasters, as in France. Often similar funding schemes exist for both film and television, but in some cases such schemes apply to one but not the other. As well as national organizations, there are transnational bodies that subsidize production in Europe. These include the Media Programme, which provides seed money, and Eurimages, which supports co-production and distribution of European film and television projects involving at least three participating countries. Domestic production is stimulated, as the public funding may be crucial to the ability to assemble a budget and in any case makes the programme or film more economically attractive to the producer and other investors.

The method of allocating subsidies varies. In many countries, including Australia and Canada, funding has to be applied for on a project-by-project basis. The government funding agency invests, often in the form of equity, in individual projects. *Ex ante* the agency funding provides downside risk protection, as it reduces the size of the loss for other investors associated with any level of revenue generation below cost, while *ex post* it provides a subsidy for projects which fail to recoup all investment costs. If government agency investments are made partially or wholly subordinate to that of other investors, the latter may recoup all of their investment while the agency bears the losses.

The project nature of this approach to funding raises the possibility, if appropriate criteria are applied, that the decision to subsidize is based on the likely external benefits generated, although this may be difficult to assess *ex ante*. However, the need to evaluate every project submitted leads to significant administrative costs.

Another approach, adopted by the CNC in France, is to provide automatic funding to eligible producers. This is less costly, but makes it impossible to tie the level and availability of subsidy to the nature of the individual project. In practice, how much of a drawback this is depends on the criteria adopted for automatic funding and the extent to which the past projects of a producer are a guide to his/her future projects. The UK lottery funding is to be awarded by the Arts Council consortia, but will not then require project-by-project assessment.

Irrespective of the approach used, incentive problems are hard to avoid. The subsidy partially insulates the producer financially from the commercial performance of the film/programme and hence lessens the motivation to be efficient. It may even facilitate the producer working for fees rather than a share of profit. If the level of potential funding is a percentage of the total project budget, this may induce budget inflation and enable broadcasters to reduce their licence fees. The Canadian experience provides some evidence of this (see Hoskins and McFadyen, 1989).

If a television programme or film is to generate external benefits it has to be watched. Thus a necessary, but not sufficient, condition for subsidy of a programme should be that a broadcaster be in place. An equivalent requirement for a feature film might be that a distributor be in place; however, it is difficult to ensure that a subsidized film achieves widespread cinema exhibition. In fact, for some countries it could be argued that the public policy stress on cinematic exhibition is misplaced. Ellis (1992) makes such an argument with respect to Canada on the basis of a comparison of the sizes of audiences reached in the various exhibition windows. A Canadian movie attracting 30,000 in cinema attendance can be expected to attract about 100,000 on pay-per-channel TV (although pay-TV is found in only 10 per cent of Canadian cable homes), about 150,000 on home video, and 1 million on broadcast TV (two showings of 500,000 each). However, one factor that Ellis fails to consider is the extent to which cinema exhibition, and the marketing and publicity surrounding it, creates a demand for the film in later exhibition windows.

Although a production subsidy is the norm for countries adopting a direct subsidy, it is questionable whether this is the optimal approach. The externalities rationale suggests that it should be consumption of the product, rather than its production, that is subsidized. Pay-per-view television would permit a government funding agency to provide a subsidy per viewer for a specific programme. Direct payment to the viewer might prove difficult, so it could be provided to the channel with the understanding it be passed onto the viewer in the form of a lower price. For feature films, vouchers or coupons could be made available for movies judged likely to result in external benefits. However, a consumption subsidy is unlikely to boost demand significantly without a marketing effort to build product awareness.

## 8.3. CONTENT REGULATIONS/QUOTAS

Many countries require that a minimum percentage of each broadcaster's programming be domestic content. In some countries, such as Australia, there is a domestic content percentage specified for various types of programming; in other countries, such as Canada, there is just an overall requirement. Classification of domestic content is typically based on a points system, with points being a weighted sum of the nationality of key inputs such as screen writer, director, producer, and main actor(s). To qualify as a domestic production a minimum number of points must be achieved. In addition, there is usually a requirement that a certain percentage of expenditures be on domestic inputs.

Such criteria seem to be very objective but, as Acheson and Maule (1990) point out, this is not always the case. For example, is news programming domestic even though portions of foreign coverage may be provided through film clips from foreign broadcasters? How do calculations of percentage expenditure treat remuneration to key personnel that is, in part, in the form of equity? Treaty co-productions with foreign partners are treated as domestic content, but how are non-treaty co-productions to be handled?

To be binding, domestic content requirements must stipulate a percentage of domestic content that is higher than the broadcaster would choose to exhibit on commercial grounds. The effect will thus be to increase the demand for domestic programming and hence the price paid. Hence, assuming no offsetting decreases in foreign demand caused by retaliatory foreign regulations, more domestic programming will be produced and it will be sold domestically at a higher price. The effect is thus of an indirect subsidy for domestic production.

Domestic content rules of this sort are not an effective way of supporting programming that provides external benefits. Whether or not external benefits are generated depends on the nature of the output, whereas content rules are based on the nationality of the inputs. As a consequence a series such as *Night Heat* was able to qualify as Canadian content although it was essentially an American story told for an American audience. As

Acheson and Maule (1990) have observed, content rules consistent with an externalities rationale might consist of a representative jury making a judgement after viewing the finished programme, in much the same way as bodies are given responsibility for classifying and censoring movies. Interactive television provides a way of implementing the Acheson and Maule suggestion.

Another problem with content rules is that their intent can be evaded. Domestic programming requirements may be satisfied primarily through low-cost productions such as game shows or repeats, or through off-peak scheduling. Given competition, content rules might be more effective if they required specific time-slots to be domestic on all channels simultaneously. Private broadcasters will always be on the lookout for ways of satisfying the letter of such rules in a manner that minimizes the impact on their profits.

In addition, new methods of dissemination are making enforcement of content regulations increasingly impractical. Video cassettes are not subject to domestic content requirements. Also, it would seem to be a losing battle to attempt to influence signals that can be received from foreign satellites or to prevent domestic audiences from viewing these signals. This has not stopped some governments from attempting to do just this. China persuaded Murdoch to drop the BBC World Service channel from its Star satellite service to that country. Putting itself in dubious company, the Canadian government is attempting, not altogether successfully, to prevent its citizens from subscribing to US direct satellite services.

## 8.4. TAX CONCESSIONS

Although tax concessions are less important than they were ten to fifteen years ago, they are still important in countries such as Ireland. They usually take the form of accelerated depreciation provisions, where the allowance can be deducted from non-film/television taxable income. Eligibility is usually based on a points system identical or similar to that used for judging domestic content. As such, this form of indirect support is subject to the same criticism as domestic content rules; the nationality of inputs is a poor guide to the nature of the final programme or film and to whether significant external benefits are generated. In addition, the project may be undertaken purely for the tax benefits, with none of the players particularly concerned with the quality of the completed programme or film or how well it sells. Indeed, tax incentives in Canada, now largely phased out, have been criticized for 'failing to provide sufficiently "good" films or sufficiently "Canadian" films' (Bird et al., 1981). In an empirical study, we found evidence that a Canadian orientation was least common amongst Canadian films released in the late 1970s and early 1980s, when tax incentives were the dominant policy strategy (Finn, Hoskins and McFadyen, 1996).

## 8.5. ENTRY BARRIERS AND LICENSING CONDITIONS

Traditionally, spectrum scarcity meant that a mechanism was needed to allocate the few available channels amongst the numerous entities wishing to offer broadcasting services. The advent of fibre-optic cable, satellite, and digital compression, however, means that spectrum scarcity is largely history. There is thus no technical need for licensing other than the house-keeping role of ensuring that signals do not interfere with one another. 'Broadcast de-regulation' is usually used to describe the increasing will-ingness of governments to increase the number of channels permitted. However, most governments still limit the number of channels in a manner that is not justified by housekeeping concerns alone.

The effect of restricting entry is that there are fewer competitors, who can hence charge a higher price; the price would be the advertising rate, a subscription rate for a pay channel, or a price per programme for a pay-per-view channel. As a result of being able to charge a higher price, the broadcaster/narrowcaster is likely to earn a higher profit than normal given the risk; economists call these excess profits 'economic profit'. Hence Lord Thompson's famous remark, in the UK context, that a television broadcast licence is 'a licence to print money'.

If the spectrum for a channel is sold by auction to the highest bidder, broadcasters' economic profits can be siphoned off. An auction was used in the allocation of the last round of ITV franchises in the UK; however, the highest bidder was not guaranteed to win, as programming promises and an ability to perform were also assessed and weighed in the franchise award decision. More commonly franchises are awarded simply on the basis of programming promises. In addition, in most coun-tries it is unheard of for an incumbent broadcaster not to have its licence renewed. The licensing process has thus provided an effective barrier to entry.

Many regulators have used their power to restrict entry to extract pro-gramming promises. In effect, a condition of the licence is a commitment that some of the expected economic profits will be spent on programming deemed desirable by the regulator. Domestic-content rules, of course, have the same effect, but specific programme hours for different types of pro-gramming and/or proportions of revenue or profits the licensee must spend are often stipulated as conditions of the licence.

We do not consider licensing conditions to be a very effective way of stimulating programming consistent with an external-benefits rationale. Broadcasters will attempt to minimize the negative impact on their profits. Promises are cheap, and in practice it has proved difficult to enforce con-ditions of licence. In many countries licences have been virtually auto-matically renewed. Even in the UK, where this has not been the case for ITV franchises, observers have remarked on the apparently tenuous rela-tionship between past programme performance and licence renewal.

## 8.6. INTERNATIONAL CO-PRODUCTION TREATIES

Many countries, the US being a major exception, have signed bilateral co-production treaties. Some, such as France and Canada, have been enthusiastic supporters of this approach, negotiating numerous treaties and actively producing under many of them. France has treaties with Algeria, Argentina, Australia, Austria, Brazil, Bulgaria, Canada, Denmark, Finland, Germany, Greece, Hungary, India, Israel, Italy, Mexico, the Netherlands, New Zealand, Poland, Portugal, Romania, Spain, Sweden, Switzerland, Tunisia, the UK, and Venezuela. Canada has negotiated more than forty treaties to encourage 'Canadian producers and their foreign counterparts to pool their creative, artistic, technical and financial resources' (Telefilm Canada, 1992: 27). Other countries, such as Japan and Australia, have been recent and apparently reluctant converts.

The treaties usually encompass both feature films and television programmes. The key principles governing these co-production agreements are typically that the minimum budget participation of a partner be 15–30 per cent of the total, that the creative and technical contribution be in proportion to the financial participation of each co-producer and/or some minimum manning level; that each producer retains revenues from its own national market while revenues from the rest of the world are normally shared in proportion to the partners' investments; and that one foreign star be permitted if both partners approve; in most cases, participation of a third country is permitted although sometimes only if the country of at least one partner has a treaty with that third country. For each agreement it is expected that over time all creative, technical, and financial contributions will be balanced.

Treaty co-productions are recognized as national productions for both partners. They qualify as domestic content for quota purposes and are eligible for investment from any government funding agency in place (usually as a percentage of the budget contribution of the home partner only), while private investors are eligible for any tax incentives.

Chapter 9 is devoted to an assessment of the co-production/co-venture strategy. However, we note here that an international co-production is an effective way to accumulate a large production budget, share other resources and experience, and learn. The ability to compete with US product is enhanced. Given this, as long as content regulations, tax incentives, and government agency funding are in place, it makes sense to have special arrangements that enable international co-productions to qualify. The fear with international co-productions is that they finish up being mid-Atlantic or 'Euro-puddings' without artistic merit or national orientation, unlikely to contribute to external benefits in the country of either of the partners. Recent experience does not support this view. In an empirical study we found that film co-productions with Canadian participation received higher critical acclaim than purely Canadian films, while there was no significant difference in perceived Canadian orientation (Finn, Hoskins and McFadyen, 1996).

## 8.7. SUMMARY AND CONCLUSION

In this chapter we have examined various approaches used to support or protect indigenous television programme and or film production. We argued that funding a public broadcasting corporation and a direct subsidy of production or, where possible, consumption are the most appropriate methods. The public broadcaster or the government agency can make investment decisions with respect to individual projects on the basis of the likely magnitude of external benefits. Content rules and licensing conditions are not as effective because they attempt to regulate conduct by forcing private broadcasters to make programme decisions that reduce profits. We agree with Harry Boyle, then chairman of the CRTC, the Canadian industry regulator, when he stated: 'there is not a regulation that has been passed that someone cannot get round if they want to' (22 Mar. 1977).

Interestingly, the US has never seriously challenged the public broadcaster and government funding agency approaches; it has instead objected strenuously to domestic content requirements, and the quota implied. But we have argued that this approach is not very effective in any case. Acheson and Maule (1990) have gone a step further, arguing that content regulations are actually detrimental to the long-run development of a programme/film production industry, on the grounds that such regulations impede development of a set of non-discriminatory international rules that would enhance the opportunity for producers in smaller countries to sell to foreign markets. Waterman (1988) makes a different case for why quotas may be detrimental, arguing that they

constrain the development of strong commercial media infrastructures by restricting the main available supply of programming needed to support expanded system capacity in the near term. In the long term, however, these commercial infrastructures must be relied upon to support domestic production activity. (1993 repr., p. 78)

# 9

# International Co-production as a Business Strategy

As we noted in Chapter 2, international co-production has become an increasingly important mode for producing both television programmes and feature films. In Western Europe in 1993, co-productions accounted for 225 of the 578 feature films produced (85 of 152 for France, 29 of 60 for the UK, and 16 of 16 for Switzerland). In Canada it was 13 of 35. In Australia, which has been relatively slow to negotiate bilateral international co-production treaties and where, prior to 1996, treaty co-productions did not automatically qualify under Australian content rules, the proportion of co-productions was only 2 of 30. For television programmes, the international co-production mode is particularly used for big-budget projects of the drama, animation, and documentary genres. An examination of Canadian television budget data 1983–91 reveals that treaty co-productions had a per-hour budget cost 2.6 times greater than the average project (Hoskins and McFadyen, 1993). International co-productions are alliances formed for individual film or television programme projects. A new corporate structure is not usually formed, but even where it is, the alliance does not take the form of an ongoing business entity.

We will use the term 'international co-production', or just 'co-production', to include any production/business arrangement, between organizations based in different countries, ranging from co-financing, where one partner's primary role is provision of a cash investment, to full co-production, where the creative, artistic, and financial contributions are roughly equal. To simplify, we will usually discuss co-productions in the context of two partners; however, often co-productions involve partners in more than two countries, or even more than one partner in a given country.

Many countries have signed bilateral international co-production treaties. Examples of countries involved and criteria for qualification were given in Chapter 8. Qualifying projects are recognized as national productions for both partners. They count as domestic content for quota purposes and are eligible for investment from any government funding agency in place (usually as a percentage of the budget contribution of the home partner only), while private investors are eligible for any tax incentives. Where we wish to refer specifically to a co-production undertaken under a bilateral treaty, we will use the term 'treaty co-production'.

International co-productions that are not undertaken under the auspices of a co-production agreement are sometimes known as 'co-ventures', but we will use the term 'non-treaty co-production'. All international co-productions with countries with which there is no treaty (notably the US) are non-treaty co-productions. Even where there is a co-production agreement, some international co-productions will not be made under its auspices. This may be because the way the project is structured does not allow it to qualify under the terms of the treaty, or because the benefits derived from having the project qualify are judged not worth the cost of the bureaucratic hurdles to be surmounted.

It is considerably more difficult for a non-treaty co-production than a treaty co-production to qualify as a domestic production for quota purposes. The non-treaty co-production must typically meet the same content and expenditure requirements as domestic productions, and the home partner must have equal decision-making responsibility for all creative elements. Rules vary with respect to eligibility for any special tax deductions and government agency funding. Twinning is a production package that pairs two distinct projects, one of which may from a creative standpoint be fully domestic and the other entirely foreign. Typically, the twins will be of the same programme category, and be of approximately equal budget and duration. The package may be undertaken under the auspices of a treaty or may be a non-treaty co-production. In this chapter we examine the benefits and drawbacks of co-producing a television programme or film. We also consider evidence with respect to the performance of co-productions and discuss the merits of use of this mode as a competitive strategy.

## 9.1. BENEFITS AND COSTS: A THEORETICAL DISCUSSION

International co-production has both advantages (benefits) and disadvantages (costs). The benefits and costs of adopting the co-production mode will be weighed against the best alternative mode and the co-production approach selected only if each partner anticipates a net benefit. Different benefits may accrue to the various partners, since the rationale for the co-production may be a pooling of complementary resources with each partner contributing a comparative advantage in a particular area.

The following potential benefits and costs have been identified from the international business literature (see e.g. Contractor and Lorange, 1988) and adapted for television programme and film production. They are discussed relative to the most frequently employed alternative, a go-it-alone domestic production.

1. *Pooling of financial resources (Financial).* Increasingly, producers are unable to raise the funds necessary for a 'world class production' from the domestic market. An international co-production may generate this level of funding through financial contributions from a foreign partner.

2. *Access to foreign government's incentives and subsidies (Fgn Subs).* If a project is structured so that it counts as domestic content in the market of each partner, it will be eligible for foreign as well as domestic government subsidies and perhaps tax incentives. As we have seen, international co-production treaties facilitate this.

3. *Access to partner's market (Part Mkt).* Improved access is likely to occur for several reasons. Firstly, the foreign partner is likely to have better knowledge regarding the distribution process in his/her domestic market and better connections to key players. Secondly, the foreign partner will have superior knowledge of the attributes demanded by viewers in his/her market and can help ensure the programme possesses such attributes. Thirdly, where quotas are in effect, a treaty co-production will qualify.

4. *Access to third-country market (Third Mkt).* The partner may enjoy superior knowledge regarding the distribution system of the third-country market and better connections with key players in it. Viewers in the third-country market may demand similar attributes (e.g. language) to those in the partner's market.

5. *Access to a project initiated by partner (Part Proj).* On occasions the main motivation for an international co-production may be to access a particular project.

6. *Cultural goals (Cultural).* Television programmes and feature films are cultural goods, and their producers may well have non-pecuniary goals.

7. *Desired foreign locations (Desired Location).* An international co-production may facilitate access to a desired foreign location. However, such access is usually possible without co-production through a service agreement whereby some services are hired at the location. For example, US producers often shoot films and programmes in Vancouver, British Columbia, using local crews but without a co-production arrangement with a Canadian partner.

8. *Cheaper inputs in partner's country (Cheaper Inputs).* An international co-production is one method of facilitating access to cheaper foreign inputs. Again, however, such access is usually available through a service agreement.

9. *Learning from partner (Learn Mktg, Learn Prod, and Learn Mgmt).* Learning opportunities may be anticipated if the partner has greater experience in programme development and marketing (Learn Mktg), in the programme or film production process (Learn Prod), or in general management (Learn Mgmt).

The joint-consumption characteristic of television programmes and films would appear to make some of these potential benefits particularly attractive. The main cost is that of producing the 'master copy', and a co-production allows several partners to pool financial resources to raise the production budget necessary. As a television programme or feature film is not 'used up' when consumed, cost is largely unaffected by the number of markets to which copies are supplied, and access to a partner's market adds revenue at very little additional cost. Similarly, the net benefits are high if the presence of the partner improves access to a third market.

The cultural discount characteristic is also relevant. In effect, the creative input of the partner should ensure that the final programme suffers a minimal discount in the partner's market, not only virtually ensuring a sale in that market but also ensuring that the sale is at a price appropriate for a domestic product rather than an import. If the partner's government operates a quota, structuring the project so that it qualifies as a domestic project in that market (this may involve structuring it as a treaty co-production) is also important in this regard. Improved access to a third market will follow if the changes made to accommodate the partner also reduce the cultural discount to the third market. For example, some French producers have used co-productions with English–Canadian producers to make a North American English-language programme or film with the hope of a sale to the US.

On the basis of this discussion, our expectation would be that financial pooling and improved access to the partner's market would be particularly important advantages, while access to a third market would be very important for some, but not all, co-productions.

While co-production has benefits, it is also likely to entail additional monetary and indirect costs. Such costs may include:

1. *Co-ordination costs (Co-ord Costs).* These are the costs of negotiating the original deal, co-ordinating production and distribution, and associated administrative burdens.

2. *Increased shooting costs (Shooting Costs).* If both partners are involved in the shooting, perhaps with shooting locations in both countries, this will likely increase costs.

3. *Loss of control and cultural specificity (Control Loss).* An international co-production inevitably involves compromises concerning the character of the programme or film and the creative talent employed. Some producers (and regulators) may be concerned that the cultural integrity of the programme or film produced is undermined. This concern is likely to have both non-monetary and monetary aspects. The programme or film may lack national orientation and may not provide external benefits. The programme/film, far from appealing to viewers in both markets, may actually appeal to neither.

4. *Increased costs of dealing with government (Gov Red Tape).* This is likely if treaty status is applied for.

5. *Opportunistic behaviour by the foreign partner (Cheating).* There is

the possibility that the partner may 'cheat' by under-allocating resources to the international co-production in the hope of a 'free ride', or by providing misleading information regarding the level of costs or revenues to be shared. However, there are considerable deterrents to such behaviour. The industry is largely run on a project basis, with an organizational mode decision for each project. Producers may anticipate being involved in a stream of such projects over time, and thus can ill afford to acquire a reputation for opportunistic behaviour. Not only are the consequences of being caught cheating serious but also, we suspect, the likelihood of the word spreading is high. This is not a secretive industry, and concerns over cheating are likely to get around to other players.

6. *Creating a more formidable competitor (Creating Competitor)*. If the foreign partner learns from collaboration in an international co-production, the expertise gained may make him/her a more formidable competitor in the future.

Given our expectation that cheating is not a major problem, co-ordination costs and costs associated with loss of control and cultural specificity would appear to be the major concerns.

## 9.2. BENEFITS AND COSTS: THE EVIDENCE

Evidence on the benefits and costs actually experienced is available from the trade literature, interviews with industry participants, and questionnaire surveys. The trade literature and interview evidence is drawn from Hoskins and McFadyen (1993).

### 9.2.1. *Trade literature evidence*

This evidence is from quotes or paraphrased statements attributed to industry participants. The quotes or paraphrased statements were drawn primarily from a systematic examination of *Playback*, the Canadian trade journal, and *Video Age International* from April 1986 to March 1990, but also draws on *Cinema Canada*, *Variety*, *Broadcaster*, and *Challenges*. Obviously some of these sources emphasize the motives of Canadian partners or foreign partners in co-productions with Canada. The results were classified by the number of occasions a benefit or drawback was mentioned, and by the country alliance context in which it was raised.

Of the potential benefits, much the most frequently cited (18 times) is pooling of financial resources. Access to the partner's market (10 citations), and access to third-country markets (9 citations) followed. In practice it was sometimes difficult to distinguish between the two, as some quotations referred to improved market access in general; on these occasions both access to the partner's market and a third country market were credited. Access to the market of the partner was mentioned most frequently (5 times) for Canadian participants in co-productions with France. The reason appears to be that treaty co-productions with France have given Canadian producers access to the French (the only sizeable market for French-language productions) and other EU markets. On the other hand, an important motive for French partners undertaking a co-production with a Canadian partner has been the hope of accessing third-country markets (4 citations), in particular the US, often through an English-language production. French producers comment approvingly that 'Canada adds a modern air' and 'the flavour is North American' (Sherman, 1987: 14).

Access to cheaper inputs and access to foreign government incentives/subsidies get several mentions. Learning and cultural goals receive few mentions. Access to a desired foreign location was not cited.

Of the costs associated with co-production, by far the most frequently mentioned is loss of control and associated cultural specificity (16 citations). The French seem particularly concerned about this in the context of partnerships with the US (6 citations). Such partnerships are looked upon as unequal, with the French partner having little control. In the words of Michel Mitrani, a prominent French producer/director, 'Co-productions with Americans invariably suffer from identity problems . . . The American determines the script. There are no compromises' (*Video Age International*, 1990: p. 41).

Increased co-ordination costs were mentioned 6 times. Not included in the count is evidence that foreigners were sometimes regarded as awkward. Brian Harris, the managing director of Yorkshire TV in the UK, is quoted as saying, 'You know the French aren't easy to deal with, and the Italians are even more difficult' (Schull and Morgan, 1989: 34), while Quebec producers are said to be exasperated by 'an arrogant but widely held perception in France that Quebec writers and actors are unable to speak international French' (Montgomery-Schell, 1989: 33).

There did not appear to be a great fear of exploitation/cheating (2 citations) or fear of creating a formidable competitor (1 mention). Fear of exploitation/cheating may be greater than this suggests, however: not included in the count were several more positively slanted statements referring to the need to select trusted foreign partners and the importance of ongoing relationships with such partners. Pat Ferns, a Canadian producer, is quoted as saying, 'It takes time to build trust, but trust is the key. People like working with partners who listen and deliver what they say' (Schull and Morgan, 1989: 34). Producers are involved in many projects over time (and often several at one time), and the discovery of cheating restricts involvement in future collaborative ventures. As Denis Heroux, the Canadian producer, states, 'If you want to seduce someone in this business, you have to realize it's not only for that night—you've got to be there the next morning too' (Wright, 1987: 37).

Overall the evidence suggests that pooling of financial resources is the most usual motive for undertaking a co-production, followed by benefits from access to a partner's market and to third-country markets. Much the most common cost identified is loss of control and cultural specificity. However, on several occasions the literature suggests a way that permits enjoyment of these advantages while avoiding this cost. The solution suggested is twinning. In the words of Stephen Roth, Canadian producer, 'Essentially there is one set of creative juices that get the project going . . . twinning is a more realistic and rewarding alternative [than traditional co-production] . . . with each producer in control of one project' (Cox, 1987: 40).

### 9.2.2. *Interview evidence*

In February 1991 interviews were conducted with seven Canadian industry participants. The primary purpose of the interviews was to obtain feedback on a proposed questionnaire on motives of co-production participants. Inevitably this led to discussions on what they considered the most important benefits and costs to be.

Uniformly they considered pooling of financial resources to be the most common and most important motive. Several mentioned that the US market had changed radically in the previous three to five years. Audience fragmentation and the associated rise of cable channels has resulted in a decrease (in real terms) in network licence fees and syndication fees and an increasing shortfall between revenues and production costs. This has led to US players seeking co-production financing.

Market access is also considered important. Canada is viewed as being in the fortunate position of constituting a bridge between Europe and the US. Europeans (particularly the French) value a Canadian partner because such a partner provides North American English and style (and the chance of a US sale) without the threat of loss of control associated with a co-production with a US partner. Americans value a Canadian partner because, through its co-production treaties, Canada can circumvent quota barriers and provide increased access to the EC market.

Depending on the exchange rate, cheaper input costs have at times been a motive for US producers seeking a Canadian partner. However, 'runaway' production, a US production shot in Canada under a service agreement, has often been used to provide this benefit without the need for a co-production.

On the cost side, loss of control received several mentions but, unlike the trade literature evidence, did not dominate increased costs associated with co-ordination and production. One producer, involved in a co-production with France, mentioned the need for daily one-hour telephone conversations with his partner. There are costs associated with keeping two sets of accounts and form-filling for two sets of bureaucracy. If double-shooting (i.e. reshooting each scene in a second language) is involved, this significantly increases costs. Different organizational cultures can cause difficulties. In Europe there is more emphasis on production as an art form rather than a business. Co-production may provide the European partner with learning opportunities, especially in the marketing area.

### 9.2.3. *Questionnaire survey evidence*

Between 1992 and 1995 we sent questionnaires, enquiring about the benefits and costs associated with using the international co-production mode, to producers in Canada, Australia, Japan, and Europe. Thirty-eight usable responses were received from producers in Canada, 37 from Australia, 18 from Japan, and 53 from Europe—26 from France, 11 from the UK, and 16 from other European countries.

For each of the potential benefits and costs listed in section 9.1, respondents were asked to indicate the importance of actual benefits received and drawbacks encountered, for the last international co-production they had completed, on a five-point Likert scale. For the questions relating to benefits: 1 = no importance, 2 = little importance, 3 = somewhat important, 4 = important, and 5 = very important. For the costs: 1 = no drawback, 2 = slight drawback, 3 = moderate drawback, 4 = significant drawback, and 5 = great drawback.

Here we report the ratings and rankings by country in general terms. Those interested in statistical tests of significance and results of project breakdowns, for example by whether the project is a television programme or feature film, are referred to Hoskins, McFadyen, Finn and Jackel (1995) for Europe and Canada, McFadyen, Hoskins, and Finn (1996) for Australia, and Hoskins, McFadyen and Finn (1997) for Japan.

Table 9.1 shows the mean (on the five-point scale) for each country for each benefit and cost item. The items are identified in the table by the abbreviation given (in parentheses) in the listing of benefits and costs in section 9.1. Although there are some differences, the ranking of importance of the benefits are generally similar for Canada, Australia, France, the UK, and other European countries. In each case the benefits from financial pooling are judged the most important, with a mean of over 4 on the five-point scale. Access to foreign government subsidies has the second highest mean for all of these countries except Australia. Improved access to the market of the partner is also viewed as important. The least important benefits are the three learning benefits and, for some countries, access to cheap inputs.

The pattern of ranking of benefits by Japanese producers is quite different. The importance of the benefit derived from financial pooling is no

TABLE 9.1.  Actual benefits and costs by country of responding partner[a]

|  | Canada | Australia | France | UK | Other European | Japan |
|---|---|---|---|---|---|---|
| *Benefits* | | | | | | |
| Financial | 4.39 | 4.56 | 4.12 | 4.64 | 4.13 | 3.88 |
| Fgn Subs | 3.37 | 2.67 | 3.50 | 4.00 | 3.81 | 2.83 |
| Part Mkt | 3.32 | 3.46 | 2.68 | 3.55 | 3.06 | 3.94 |
| Third Mkt | 2.37 | 2.49 | 2.42 | 3.00 | 1.87 | 3.29 |
| Cultural | 2.32 | 2.70 | 2.61 | 2.18 | 2.47 | 3.89 |
| Part Proj | 2.30 | 2.51 | 2.42 | 2.46 | 1.88 | 3.00 |
| Cheap Inputs | 2.19 | 1.92 | 2.68 | 2.00 | 1.53 | 3.00 |
| Location | 2.13 | 2.61 | 2.79 | 3.00 | 2.20 | 3.94 |
| Learn Mkt'g | 1.82 | 2.11 | 1.64 | 1.64 | 1.75 | 3.06 |
| Learn Prod | 1.54 | 1.67 | 1.84 | 1.73 | 1.63 | 3.28 |
| Learn Mgmt | 1.37 | 1.63 | 1.40 | 1.73 | 1.44 | 2.72 |
| *Costs* | | | | | | |
| Co-ord Costs | 3.21 | 3.30 | 3.12 | 2.91 | 3.25 | 2.88 |
| Shooting Costs | 2.66 | 2.65 | 2.81 | 1.73 | 2.94 | 2.47 |
| Control Loss | 2.39 | 2.34 | 2.62 | 2.55 | 1.88 | 3.00 |
| Gov Red Tape | 2.51 | 2.35 | 2.32 | 1.82 | 2.13 | 2.20 |
| Cheating | 2.11 | 2.08 | 2.12 | 2.30 | 3.06 | 2.94 |
| Creating Competitor | 1.71 | 1.64 | 1.44 | 1.36 | 1.53 | 1.19 |

[a] Benefits ranking: 1 = no importance; 5 = very important. Costs ranking: 1 = no drawback; 5 = great drawback.

*Source*: Questionnaire survey data collected by the authors for Canada, Australia and Japan, and by Anne Jackel and the authors for France, the UK, and other European nations.

longer dominant. Its mean of 3.88 puts it into a group with access to partner's market, access to foreign location, and cultural benefits. Relative to other countries, it appears that the financial pooling benefit is less important, but these other benefits are more important. Also very noticeable is the higher level of importance attributed to each of the learning benefits.

With respect to costs of choosing the international co-production mode, there are again some obvious differences between Japan and the other countries. Canada, Australia, France, the UK, and other European countries all rank coordination costs as the largest drawback. Loss of control is less important. Japanese producers, on the other hand, report means for loss of control and cheating that are similar to that for coordination costs. The drawback associated with cheating is also considered important in the other European nations group, but is given low importance by Canada, Australia, France, and the UK.

The relative importance of the benefits reported for the Western nations are much as we would expect on the basis of our theoretical discussion and largely consistent with the trade literature and interview evidence. Financial pooling is the most important benefit, while improved access to partner's market also figures prominently. Somewhat surprisingly, given that this item received little stress in the trade literature or interviews (perhaps producers do not wish to publicize this motive), access to foreign subsidies is rated as an important benefit.

We believe that many of the differences in responses observed between Japanese producers and producers in the West can be explained in terms either of cultural distance or of Japan's management culture. Both the Japanese and Western responses relate primarily to co-productions with producers from the West. The Japanese are thus more culturally distant from their partners. Increased cultural distance results in a larger cultural discount for a domestic programme or film that is exported. Reduction of this cultural discount through use of the co-production mode is thus likely to result in substantial benefits in terms of improved market access; it is no wonder that improved access to a partner's market and a third market are more important benefits to Japanese producers. However, increased cultural distance may lead to misunderstandings, and it is not surprising that Japanese producers typically give more weight to costs associated with loss of control and cheating. Japanese management culture has always emphasized the importance of learning, so it is consistent to find that Japanese producers report greater benefits associated with learning. We have developed these thoughts further elsewhere in a statistical analysis of the differences in the responses of Japanese and Canadian respondents (see Hoskins, McFadyen and Finn, 1997).

## 9.3. EVIDENCE ON PERFORMANCE

The questionnaires also asked producers to rate performance on a five-point scale. Several dimensions of performance were identified; financial success in terms of recoupment of total project costs, financial success in terms of own organization's participation, project creative/artistic success, and overall project success. Our research on performance is ongoing, but we have preliminary results from an analysis of responses for Canadian producers in co-productions with a European partner (35 responses) and of European producers in co-productions with a Canadian partner (26 responses).

The overall performance rating is more than satisfactory. However, it appears this is only because a good creative/artistic performance outweighs a less than satisfactory total project recoupment. Generally, Canadian partners seem more satisfied than European. The main source of the difference appears to relate to Canada–France English-language projects. As we have seen, the trade literature evidence suggests that the main motive for French producers in such projects is to achieve a look acceptable to US viewers. Our questionnaire results suggest that French producers may have been disappointed in this regard.

## 9.4. SUMMARY AND CONCLUSION

International co-productions have become an increasingly important mode. This is not surprising, since international co-production is a strategy that takes advantage of the joint-consumption and cultural discount characteristics of television programmes and films. It permits partners to pool finance to raise the substantial budget required to produce the 'master copy' which can then be reproduced at minimal cost to supply additional markets. Access to the partner's market, and perhaps to a third market, is greatly improved, as the partner's market knowledge and creative input are used to eliminate, or at least minimize, the cultural discount. Consistent with this, the evidence suggests that financial pooling is the dominant benefit for producers in Canada, Australia, France, the UK, and other European countries, while access to the partner's market is also important. The responses of Japanese producers are quite different. The importance of financial pooling is no longer dominant, while learning benefits are rated much higher than they are by Western producers. These differences, and others identified, can be explained in terms of cultural distance or Japan's management culture.

The evidence presented on performance is limited to Canada–Europe co-productions. While the overall performance rating is more than satisfactory, this is largely a reflection of a good creative/artistic performance. This is somewhat ironic, as creative/artistic performance has traditionally been the popular concern with complaints of 'Euro-puddings' or 'Mid-Atlantic' programmes and films. This concern does seem to have largely abated in recent years, however.

Producers may not always eagerly embrace the co-production mode; it adds cost, complexity, and a need to compromise. However, it is often the only strategy which permits producers, aside from the US majors, to accumulate the large budgets necessary to produce films and programmes that can compete effectively on the international market. As television audiences, including those in the US itself, continue to fragment, the co-production mode can be expected to become even more important.

# Business Issues and Strategies

The film and television industries are entertaining in many more ways than one. Not only do most people enjoy consuming these products, but almost as many people are interested in how these industries operate, judging from the success of TV programmes like *Entertainment Tonight* and books like *Fatal Subtraction*. We have already seen that the economic characteristics of their products makes these industries different, but what is it about the management of these industries that makes them so interesting? Why does a superstar earn $20 million for one movie? Why do we expect Fox to release *Independence Day III: More of the Same* even if *Independence Day II: Let's Do It Again* fails to achieve the box office revenue of the original *Independence Day*? Why are international markets moving towards simultaneous international releasing? Why is everyone you meet in Hollywood either writing a script or shooting a TV pilot? How can a movie take in $100 million at the box office without reporting a profit? In this chapter, which addresses some of the marketing and managerial principles that underlie the performance of firms in these industries, we provide answers to these and similar questions.

To address such questions we need to understand (i) the structure and management of organizations that require both creative and business skills to function effectively, and (ii) the extraordinary degree of uncertainty about consumer demand and consequent strategies for handling the resulting risk. In this chapter we briefly examine each of these issues, and then investigate how they can account for the well-known peculiarities found in the management of audiovisual industry businesses. The explanations are based on developments in the academic disciplines of management, organizational analysis, marketing and distribution, new product development, managerial economics, accounting, and finance. Our discussion draws on Finn, McFadyen and Hoskins (1994).

## 10.1. THE ELUSIVENESS OF ARTISTIC CREATIVITY AND INGREDIENTS FOR SUCCESS

Creativity is an extraordinarily elusive concept. As a consequence, it is extremely difficult to provide an environment which recognizes and fosters creativity whilst maintaining the market discipline necessary to achieve commercial objectives. Litwak (1986: 55) describes the problem as follows:

Hollywood is a town divided into two camps: creative and business—each suspicious of the other. Writers, directors and artists are members of the creative community. According to the businessmen, creative types are wonderfully talented people but, like children, cannot be trusted with money. On the other hand, says the creative community, studio executives, producers and agents are businessmen who are concerned only with making money and have no taste or artistic sensibility.

As more and more film and television markets are opened to competitive pressures, industry organizations cannot afford to focus exclusively on creative and artistic achievement. To survive and prosper, creative ideas must be transformed into commercially successful films or programmes.

### 10.1.1. Why is it musical chairs in the Hollywood studio executive suite?

An issue like this falls within the domain of the fields of organizational analysis and the industrial organization area of economics. All cultural industries have a highly skilled labour force, one with hands-on production experience and the collective creative ability to generate new products to keep pace with changing market demands. Workers in these industries have knowledge that is both specialized and fungible, that is not limited to an individual task but applicable to a wide range of activities. The organizations that elicit the best performance from such workers (i.e. that best complement these human capital inputs) are highly porous—with boundaries that are ill-defined, where work roles are evolving and responsibilities overlapping, and where work ties, both across teams and to members of other organizations, are strong. Shifting to a network type of organization both changes the internal organization of firms and revamps their relationships with trading partners. Realignments include new cooperative relationships with suppliers in such areas as production, marketing, and distribution, as well as research and development collaborations.

The feature film and television programme production industries rely heavily on subcontracting and freelance talent. The industry thrives on short-term contracts, minimization of fixed overheads, mutual monitoring of buyers and sellers, and a constant weaving and interweaving of project credits, relationships, and successes or failures. It is often the network of personal relationships between participants that is stable and enduring, not the film studio in which the participants work. Studio employees, from top to bottom, and occasionally studios (such as United Artists and Ealing) come and go. Even when they stay, ownership changes frequently, as in the case of MGM. Smart executives can generate a studio's wave of success, lucky executives can ride the wave to a crest, but the smartest executives bale out before its crash.

Christopherson and Storper (1986; 1989) have described the evolution of film production from a craft industry, modelled on the live theatre in New York, through large vertically integrated studios in Hollywood employing industrial mass production methods (Fordism) to flexible specialism (post-Fordism). They argue that the high fixed costs associated with mass production could not be justified after the increase in demand uncertainty caused by the Paramount Decision of 1948, which required studios to divest themselves of their theatre holdings, and the spread of television, which led to a 50 per cent decline in cinema audiences between 1946 and 1956.

Activities that had been within the studio framework gradually moved to the external market. Eventually, this meant the complete end of the 'term contract', under which writers, actors, and skilled production people worked exclusively for one studio for a specified period of time. It was replaced by a film-to-film contract. (Christopherson and Storper, 1986: 309)

Consequences have been to reduce the Hollywood majors' advantage in production and to facilitate shooting outside Hollywood, in part to avoid restrictive work practices.

Aksoy and Robins (1992) have criticized Christopherson and Storper for concentrating on organizational solutions to minimizing transactions costs associated with production. They argue that this emphasis on production is unfortunate when 'what distinguishes the film industry . . . is the crucial importance of distribution and exhibition' (1992: 7). Because of their continued control of distribution and finance, the power of the Hollywood majors has not eroded. In a rejoinder, Storper (1993) maintains that their argument, that the move to flexible specialization reduced the Hollywood majors' competitive edge in production, never implied vertical disintegration and loss of control of distribution.

### 10.1.2. *How do you get 'suits' to work well with 'flakes'?*

The general management literature helps us understand how best to manage organizations that require both creative and business skills to function. Here, as in other industries, there are some different approaches to doing business. According to the marketing concept, the key is to first determine the needs and wants of a target market and then to deliver these more effectively and efficiently than competitors. Specifically, the marketing concept combines four elements: a market focus, a customer orientation, coordinated marketing, and a goal of profitability.

Although now widely accepted in business, the marketing concept has not been unopposed. Many participants in the cultural industries adhere to competing views of the way organizations should conduct their business, including the production concept, product concept, and selling concept. Nevertheless, in other industries the marketing concept has always eventually supplanted these competing views. Adherents of the production concept think consumers will favour those products which are widely available and low in cost. Thus, production-oriented organizations concentrate on achieving production efficiency. However, this approach is only successful when the demand for a product far exceeds the supply, so that customers are satisfied just to obtain the product. Advocates of the product concept assume that consumers will always favour products offering more quality, performance, and features. In product-oriented organizations, which are common in television and especially in film, managers focus their energy on making high-quality products and finding new ways to improve them over time. However, product-oriented managers often become over-enamoured with their product improvements. As a result, they fail to appreciate that the customer may not be able to detect marginal improvements, and may not be prepared to pay for other real improvements in quality, performance, or features. Finally, adherents to the selling concept think that consumers, if left alone, will not buy enough of the organization's product(s), so their organizations have to undertake aggressive selling and promotion efforts. Managers in these organizations aim to sell whatever it is they make, rather than recognizing that they could make what would sell.

As an industry becomes more open and competitive, transition to the marketing concept becomes more critical for organizational success or even survival. Still, there continues to be resistance, pronounced in some cultural industries, to allowing a focus on satisfying customer needs to direct an organization's activities. For example, Hirschman (1983) argues that the marketing concept, as a normative framework, is not applicable to artists because artists create primarily to express their subjective conceptions of beauty, emotion or some other aesthetic ideal. Their creativity is expressed for its own sake, and the creative process itself is intrinsically satisfying. According to this view, such artists differ from creators of utilitarian products in that their creativity is valued for its expressive qualities, and not strictly for its functional utility or technical competence. Clearly, such artists do not accept the marketing concept; they can be viewed as representing an extreme version of the product orientation. There will always be participants in the cultural industries who wish to remain pure artists and hence cannot accept the marketing concept. But to the extent that artists do not care if they communicate with an audience, the legitimacy of their claim on public funds to satisfy their desires must be compromised.

To implement the marketing concept, a continuous programme of consumer research is necessary to monitor consumer needs and changing interests and to guide managers in their strategic and operational decision making. Because it has traditionally sold access to its audience to advertisers, the television industry has historically devoted significant levels of resources to consumer research. They have conducted consumer research to satisfy the demands of advertisers who require detailed information on the audience they reach. Much of this research has involved collecting behavioural data on who is viewing, and what these viewers do and buy. Such data has usually been collected by independent media research companies. In addition, some broadcasters have been early adopters of customer satisfaction and service quality research. As inter-industry competition increases, it will be necessary for firms to pay more attention to customer satisfaction and how it affects customers' perceptions of firms' overall service quality.

### 10.1.3. *Why does every project need a producer when it already has a director?*

This is a project management issue. Just as a firm requires a successful integration of creative and business inputs, so does each and every project. In film and television production, the relationship between the director and the producer encapsulates these roles. It is easy for creativity to run off into the clouds, conjuring up novel stories and images that no one wants to see. On the other hand, not many audiences want to watch a monotone presentation of an itemized budget, statements of cost variances, projected profit and loss, and a detailed marketing and distribution plan. Throughout every project, success requires a balancing of the creative and the business imperative. While a few blockbusters have arisen from projects where one person acts as both director and producer, few people have the capacity to walk the tightrope from idea to market, balancing both roles.

### 10.2. UNCERTAINTY ABOUT CONSUMER DEMAND AND STRATEGIES FOR HANDLING THE RESULTING RISK

Film and television programmes typically have relatively short life cycles. Thus industry participants must continually generate new products. But each really new product can be unique, risky, and involve high up-front costs. Production budgets in the millions, or even tens of millions, of dollars are often committed based on an assessment of a script and the identity of some key participants (producer, scriptwriter, director, and actors), long before there is any information about the likely market interest in the specific project. And in general we know demand is extremely variable. A Hollywood blockbuster such as *Independence Day* can make over $200 million in North American box office, whereas another movie with similar costs can open at as many theatres and flop, taking in only one or two million. Revenues for firms can also vary widely; thus quarterly revenues of Castle Rock plummeted from $67 million in 1995 to $39 million in 1996. The fallibility of even the Hollywood majors in predicting success is illustrated by the many industry hits turned down by various studios, including *Star Wars*, *Back to the Future*, *Driving Miss Daisy*, and *Dances with Wolves*.

Cultural industry organizations need processes which can translate creative ideas into commercially successful products. In other industries, new product researchers (Cooper, 1980; Cooper and Kleinschmidt, 1990) have sought the secret of new product success in the characteristics of (i) the new product itself, (ii) the new product development process, and (iii) the market environment. The most important finding has been that the factors most strongly associated with success are generally those most amenable to management action. In contrast, success is not nearly as strongly associated with non-controllable or situational factors, such as market competitiveness, market potential, marketing synergy, and technological synergy (Cooper and Kleinschmidt, 1990; Hise et al., 1990).

There is no magic formula that a producer can apply to consistently turn out successes, but cross-sectional studies have investigated how the characteristics of a finished movie (Litman, 1983; Smith and Smith, 1986; Wyatt, 1994) and the specialization of business and creative roles (Baker and Faulkner, 1991) have influenced the box office performance of US films. For example, Wallace, Seigerman and Holbrook (1993) found that the presence of one of the leading stars accounted for about 15 per cent of the variance in US film rentals, while Baker and Faulkner (1992) found that the most successful Hollywood adaptation to the blockbuster era has been the development of film projects where the business side is handled by a specialist producer, and the creative side is characterized by the star also serving as director. We are engaged in similar research on Canadian movies and television programmes. In addition, numerous studies provide the useful case specific details lost in such statistical analyses (e.g. Daly, 1980; Rosen, 1990; Posner, 1993).

Marketing has come to play an increasingly important role, with the realization that producers need to do everything in their power to ensure there is sufficient market demand for their projects to be economically successful. Besides the acceptance of the marketing concept, a successful marketing approach requires an understanding of the entertainment and information needs of potential market segments, the identification of a market segment to target, and the development of an appropriate product offering and marketing mix for the targeted segment. A popular classification of the elements of the marketing mix is known as 'the four Ps': product, price, place (i.e., distribution), and promotion.

*10.2.1. Does anyone really watch* The Kung-Fu Shark Meets
the Boston Strangler, Extreme Sports Bloopers,
*and the Home Shopping Channel?*

The marketing concept suggests that success will be achieved by organizations which focus their efforts on developing a marketing mix that best meets the needs of consumers. However, markets are composed of consumers with a variety of different needs. As consumer needs vary, one marketing mix cannot adequately meet the needs of the entire market. On the other hand, if the marketer can divide the total market into subgroups of consumers, who themselves have homogeneous needs, then the marketer can provide a separate marketing mix for each of these segments. The result is that the needs of all are closer to being fully satisfied. The choice and implementation of a specific marketing mix, which is designed to satisfy a segment, is referred to as 'positioning the product for the segment'.

Film and television markets can be segmented on demographic, socioeconomic, geographical lines, and in terms of social class, lifestyle, product usage, attitudes and perceptions, benefits, and usage situation differences between consumers (Wind, 1978). Sometimes a single consumer characteristic is the basis for the segment's existence: it is essentially the reason why the group of consumers responds differently to the same marketing mix. Young children are not only identified by their age: their age makes them respond favourably to the same simpler story-line and repetitive presentation that will annoy teenagers. These are identifiable groups who are different, who will respond differently to the same television programme. Use of a segmentation strategy requires segments which are identifiable, accessible, of substantive size, and responsive (Nylen, 1990). In analysing segmentation strategies, it is relevant to consider the response of viewers, as well as of the broadcaster or other actual purchaser, to the attributes provided. Implementation requires selection of the target audience segment and positioning of the offering to attract members of the target segment. Farley (1986) states that 'international marketers are often so preoccupied with observable differences in the markets that they serve that they fail to grasp similarities in consumer response across markets'. Grounds for such similarities can be identified across different national markets and provide the opportunity for standardization based on serving cross-national segments.

US action/conflict drama, in feature film and television series form, reaches the 12–25 age group in many countries. Action drama is expensive to make, however, and some producers may find a smaller cross-country segment more attractive. The mass market targeted by much of the US drama tends to be of lower educational/socioeconomic status. This leaves a niche for producers, such as the BBC, to target viewers in higher groups through programmes like historical drama and documentaries. Anglia, a small regional company in the UK's commercial ITV network, has established a position producing wildlife and nature programming. The very language/cultural differences that normally act as barriers may provide niche opportunities for selling productions to ethnic markets in other countries. For example, an Italian producer can sell Italian-language programmes and films to multilingual stations in New York, Sydney, and Toronto. Video cassettes are also a good way to access ethnic markets (see Hoskins and McFadyen, 1986). Further examples of the segmentation strategy are provided by Hoskins and McFadyen (1991a).

### 10.2.2. *Why make* Independence Day III: More of the Same *even if* Independence Day II: Let's Do It Again *is not a success?*

Because *Independence Day* was a blockbuster in 1996, we know that we can expect a sequel in 1998, and even if that does not do particularly well we are still likely to see Part III released in the year 2000.

As noted earlier, the revenue a producer of films or television programmes will make from introducing a new product is extremely difficult to predict. The risk is extraordinarily high. One way of reducing the uncertainty when developing new film and television programming projects is the use of sequels to successful products that continue with the same characters and type of story-line as the original. Examples abound in feature films. Feature films based on the James Bond books of Ian Fleming were so successful that other authors were commissioned to write sequels after Fleming's death. The original *Star Wars* trilogy was an unprecedented success; a new trilogy is planned with tentative release dates of 1999, 2001, and 2003. Interestingly, *Star Wars* illustrates another ploy for minimizing risk. *Star Wars: The Special Edition* was released in 1997. Some new visuals have been added, but this is essentially a release of the 1977 film. The cost of the release is reported to be $10 million, about one-third of the cost of a new Hollywood film (with unproven market appeal).

The television equivalent of the sequel is the series itself. Sequels and series build on a successful format, are less demanding for the consumer, who already knows the characters, and attempt to build a loyal following. They also possess a cost advantage, as they already have characters and plots developed and actors in place. For a successful series, however, at least some of the cost advantage may be lost when the series is renewed, as stars, such as those of *Friends*, negotiate higher salaries. *Star Trek* provided the platform for *Star Trek: The Next Generation*, and more recently *Star Trek: Deep Space Nine*, so sequels are also developed for television series. Promoting brand loyalty for stand-alone films or single-episode programmes is harder, but can be attempted by packaging them under anthology headings such as 'Masterpiece Theatre' or 'Mystery!'. Developing clones of popular series, cross-pollination of characters between series, and the spinning-off of characters to produce new series obviously have some of the advantages of sequels.

So now we know why *Part II: Let's Do it Again* was made, but then why make *Part III: More of the Same* if Part II is not a success? Well, of course, it turns out that Part II is typically only seen as a failure when judged relative to the blockbuster success of the original. Even if a sequel produces only a half as much box office as its predecessor, and Part III is expected to drop a further 50 per cent, its expected revenue is probably still far higher than what we would expect for the alternative—a randomly presented script that is competing for the studio's funds.

### 10.2.3. *Why can a superstar earn $20 million for one movie?*

The revenue of producers of films and television programmes is inherently unstable because they are continually introducing new products whose success is difficult to predict. Ryan (1991) argues that one important role of marketing in the management of cultural products is to reduce the uncertainty associated with the audience's reaction to creative efforts. Marketing activities help stabilize demand by positioning creative efforts in the consumers' recognizable conceptual space of stars and styles. Brand loyalty may to a greater or lesser extent be attached to the actor (feature films and television programmes), or director (feature films). The Hollywood star system is an attempt to establish brand loyalty and promote high, stable revenues. Rosen (1981) shows that as the size of the below-the-line budget increases, so does the need for risk reduction strategies, and the amount the producer might offer the risk-reducing star. Thus the *share* of total cost going to above-the-line creative costs increases as the below-the-line costs rise. So while the star of an Australian movie with a budget of $3 million makes $30,000 (1 per cent), the star of the Hollywood movie with a budget of $40 million makes $10 million (25 per cent).

Ironically, the economic forces which make it worthwhile for the Hollywood studios to offer an established international superstar a fee as high as $20 million to make a single movie means that stars nurtured in smaller national industries, such as Gérard Depardieu from France or Mel Gibson from Australia, are attracted to Hollywood. Once co-opted into the central system, they reinforce its relative strength.

### 10.2.4. *Why is Hollywood so enamoured with blockbusters?*

*Star Wars*, released in 1977, earned a then unprecedented box office of $325 million. It is usually credited with beginning the era of the special effects blockbuster. Blockbusters have several advantages for the Hollywood majors. The blockbuster becomes almost a brand name in itself. Blockbusters are easy to promote and sell as 'high concept' (Wyatt, 1994). They are particularly attractive to the 12–24-year-olds that make up the prime movie theater audience; and they lend themselves to merchandising. The special effects become the stars and can, at least partially, reduce the need for expensive star actors. For example, the three lead actors in *Star Wars* were not well known when the film was released, although Harrison Ford later became a star. The two lead actors of the 1996 release *Twister* were not established movie stars. Nevertheless, the expense of the special effects themselves makes it difficult for non-Hollywood producers to compete in this genre.

### 10.2.5. *Why did E.T. love Reese's Pieces?*

Placement and merchandising are now important sources of revenue. Wasko (1994: 188–9) estimates that product placements alone can easily bring in more than $1 million per film (based on 20–50 placement opportunities sold for $5,000–250,000 each). E.T. loved Reese's Pieces because the Hershey Company paid for product placement. The Hershey Company loved *E.T.: The Extra Terrestrial* because the placement is credited with increasing sales of Reese's Pieces by 85 per cent.

Merchandising involves the direct sale of products based on the characters or themes of the movie, such as X-Wing Fighters, Ninja Turtles, and video games based on *Last Action Hero*. Merchandising opportunities are no longer treated as an additional revenue opportunity after completion of the movie. Indeed, 'video games . . . are developed and produced simultaneously with a feature film. The majors now have video game components [*sic*] or subsidiaries, which check out the potential of new films for game versions, may even alter film scripts to make more exciting games, and shoot footage for games at the same time the film is shot' (Wasko, 1994: 210).

### 10.2.6. *Why a special premiere for horses at a Los Angeles drive-in?*

Publicity plays a far more important role in the promotional mix for films and television programmes than in other industries, and it is often more important than advertising (Rubin, 1992). Many of the most famous publicity stunts were created by Hollywood studios to help promote movies, including Marty Weiser's favourite stunt, which attracted more than 250 horses and riders, and the all-important media, for a showing of *Blazing Saddles* (Fuhrman, 1989). Moreover, the advertising and sales promotion elements of the mix often involve the use of cross-promotion with other cultural products, such as movies with their soundtracks or book versions, and tie-in promotions with producers of other consumer products (Wyatt, 1994). The other consumer products can do well even when the cultural product is a comparative failure, as Daly (1980) notes when discussing the 1974 movie version of *The Great Gatsby*.

The industry is unusual in that even seemingly negative publicity is likely to be good for business. Media controversy has historically proved highly effective in creating awareness of films and TV programmes which might otherwise have only attracted a niche audience.

### 10.2.7. *Why does every theatre complex show the same set of eight movies?*

It is important to identify the optimal distribution strategy for a film—how best to capitalize on the potential audience and the differing reservation prices amongst this audience.

The alternative theatrical release patterns for movies have different time profiles of distribution intensity. In the pre-blockbuster era, distribution intensity would typically increase over time. Movies were usually given an exclusive first run in one theatre per regional market, followed by a second run at a number of theatres, before finally going to wide release in the regional market. This strategy facilitated the use of a price discrimination policy, with first-run theatres able to charge higher prices. In addition, by relying on word-of-mouth recommendations, it minimized advertising expenses. Now, most US blockbuster movies are given saturation television advertising and concentrated publicity to generate high levels of awareness before opening simultaneously in all North American regional markets. These movies usually have their widest distribution in the first week of release, with the intensity declining over successive weeks as the box office volume declines. Both Inman and Wheat (1992) and Krider and Weinberg (1992) found that they could model a movie's weekly box office receipts by assuming that receipts declined exponentially from a peak in the first week of release. This wide release pattern, with its high first-weekend box office figures, also helps generate excitement amongst all members of the cultural production system.

Because of the high print and advertising costs, and consequent high risks involved, few non-Hollywood movies have attracted the distributor confidence and exhibitor support necessary to use this wide-release blockbuster strategy. Most continue to rely on exclusive openings or a regional roll-out from market to market.

As publicity increasingly spills over international boundaries, through such vehicles as international news services, studio home pages on the World Wide Web, and promotional and licensing arrangements with worldwide consumer products companies such as McDonald's and Hasbro, it becomes increasingly attractive to release movies which are expected to do very well simultaneously rather than sequentially across international markets.

As marketing expenses rise relative to the cost of production, there are advantages to amortizing them more quickly over a larger total market.

Higher production budgets, higher ratios of marketing expenses to production costs, faster international diffusion of entertainment industry news and publicity, and the substantial savings in print costs as electronic methods of delivering films become more widely used will reinforce this trend. In an example of extreme publicity spill-over, namely US movies in Canada, as discussed earlier, the US studios prefer to treat Canada as just another part of the US market.

### 10.2.8. Why do we wait so long for new movies to appear in the video store?

Of course, first-run theatrical release is only the first release window for a movie. The joint-consumption good cost structure makes it attractive for suppliers to extend market reach. Windowing extends market reach through sequencing sales to different markets through time. Windowing, a form of price discrimination, is an attractive business strategy because the product is not used up by consumption and hence can be resold to different markets over time at little addition to cost. As long as the incremental revenue brought in is greater than the small increment to cost, sales to an additional market are worthwhile. One can now identify as many as eight release windows for feature films in some geographical markets; first-run theatre exhibition, second-run theatre (dollar movies), pay-per-view, home video, premium cable (movie channels), network television, re-release to basic cable, and television syndication.

Some of these would also apply to television programming. Occasionally a feature film version for cinema release is edited from the shoot of a television mini-series. Examples include the Canadian mini-series *Bethune* and *Joshua Then and Now*. Where the feature film version is well received, the cinema exposure acts as very effective promotion for the video and broadcast mini-series versions that follow. The satellite channels in Europe open up the possibility of selling exhibition rights to some very old television series. *My Favorite Martian*, a moderately successful US fantasy series shown on CBS in 1963–5, was some twenty-five years later exhibited by Sky Channel.

Owen and Wildman (1992: 30) identify six factors that a windowing strategy, designed to maximize profits from all distribution channels, must consider:

(1) differences in the per viewer price earned in the different distribution channels; (2) differences in channels' incremental audiences . . . (3) the interest rate as a measure of the opportunity cost of money; (4) the extent to which viewers exposed to a program through one channel are eliminated from its potential audience in other channels; (5) differences among channels in their vulnerability to unauthorized copying; and (6) the rate at which viewer interest in a program declines following its initial release.

All of these factors must be weighed in determining the optimal sequencing and length of the various windows, and even whether a potential window should be included or excluded.

Owen and Wildman seem to view the different windows as competing for the audience. However, they may also in some cases be complementary. The video window for feature films is now bigger than the cinema release window, and it may well be that a successful cinema release boosts the audience in the video window and perhaps other, later windows; in effect it is advertising or promotion for the later windows.

Production decisions increasingly reflect the multiple windows a film project is targeting. They thus reflect broadcast and video cassette exhibition possibilities, as well as international sales possibilities. As Wasko reports, script decisions and selection of actors are influenced by how the movie will play 'not only Peoria but in Pisa, Perth and, now, Prague' (1994: 236).

### 10.2.9. *How come video purchase prices were $80 one year and $20 the next?*

We examined the export pricing of television programmes in Chapter 5, so we confine our observations here to film and video. Surprisingly little research has been reported on optimal pricing of cultural products. Sensitivity to price varies; however, it appears that the demand for a particular new movie at the cinema is not very sensitive to the price charged. On the other hand, the prevalence and longevity of 'Cheap Tuesday' at North American cinemas indicates that the difference in price elasticity between days of the week is sufficient to make this form of price discrimination profitable.

In the early 1990s the price of video cassettes to consumers was reduced from around $80 to $20 or less. As this change in price has been maintained, we can assume it was profitable. For this to be the case the revenue from sales must have increased, which implies that the percentage increase in sales of cassettes was greater than the percentage decrease in price (a price elasticity of greater than one in economic terminology). As we noted in Chapter 3, some of this increase in legal sales would probably come from people forsaking pirate copies. Not only must revenue from sales have increased, but the increase in revenue must have exceeded the increase in cost due to the need to supply more cassettes (the low incremental cost of producing cassettes would have kept this additional cost low), and any reduction in revenue to the producer from other windows.

### 10.2.10. *Why is everyone in Hollywood either writing a script or shooting a TV pilot?*

The new product development process consists of five major stages: idea generation, concept testing, product development, pre-launch market testing, and market introduction. At each stage the managerial problem is to identify from the flow of projects (with variable expected production and marketing costs) those to be rejected, those to be reworked and reconsidered, and those to be forwarded to the next stage, in order to obtain an optimal portfolio of products. At each stage a proportion of what were thought to be viable projects fall by the wayside, as new types of shortcoming are identified. A proactive approach to idea generation is important, because the more ideas that are actively considered before it is decided which one to develop, the more likely there is to be an attractive idea available to be chosen. This translates into an emphasis on script development in the film and television programme production industry.

The Hollywood majors have increasingly used the negative pick-up as a low-cost, low-risk method of maintaining a flow of films to their distribution arm. The major agrees to pay a share of the production cost on delivery of the film negative. If the film is not completed, no payment is made. Concept testing uses low-cost consumer responses to eliminate ideas which have little chance of market success before much money is spent. It has long been used for films and US network television. For film, it may be useful to also conduct concept tests on distributors and critics, whose reactions may be just as important to success. The further into the product development process, the more useful the test—thus a test based on a completed script should predict better than one based on a pure concept statement.

Pre-launch market testing is more valuable for projects with high launch costs, such as films. Its applicability may be greater for products which are typically experienced once, such as movies and television programmes, than for products which are experienced repeatedly, where evaluations may change with repeated exposures. One common form of pre-launch market testing, pilot testing, is widely used for film (Austin, 1989) and television (Stipp and Schiavone, 1990). It can be used to guide final editing, to identify target segments, and to choose promotional themes. Paramount is reported to have shot a new ending for *Fatal Attraction* because test audiences gave the original a thumbs down (Diamond, 1989). Even then the same ending was not used in all markets; in Japan the movie ended with a suicide.

The market introduction of a new cultural product requires the use of standard consumer marketing research techniques, such as focus groups and surveys, to develop an appropriate marketing mix. For films, Austin (1989) reviews work on testing alternative titles, determining what aspects are most appealing, positioning for promotional purposes, designing trailers, and media selection.

So why is everyone writing a script? Obviously, producers need the pool of ideas being developed into scripts to be extremely large—not only does this increase the odds of a gem being out there to be discovered, it reduces the chance of writers extracting the same surplus as stars.

*10.2.11. How can a movie make $100 million at the box office without making a profit?*

Much of the discussion of accounting in the feature film industry revolves around the issue of whether the studios indulge in creative accounting to appropriate resources properly due to artists working on the pictures (see e.g. O'Donnell and McDougal, 1992).

As we saw in Chapter 5, the Hollywood majors are vertically integrated. They are in distribution as well as production. It is the profits of the studio as a whole that are important, and if the contract of the director or a lead actor stipulates a share of the profit on the production, then it may be better that the distribution arm realizes all the profits on a particular project. Prindle (1993: 22–3) provides an example. The worldwide box office receipts for *Coming to America* were $250 million. The theatres retained half of this, leaving Paramount, which produced and distributed the film, with revenues of $125 million. Nevertheless, the production arm of Paramount showed a net loss of $15 million after deducting production costs of $57 million, distribution and marketing costs of $36 million, interest of $5 million, and (and this is the key) a distribution fee of $42 million to its own distribution arm.

Litwak (1986) suggests that much of the criticism of the studios for indulging in creative accounting is misfocused. It is the unequal terms of the agreements originally entered into, not the accounting, which is to be criticized. Moreover, those terms simply reflect relative market power at the time when the agreement was signed. Typically, the creator who feels hard done by has effectively signed away the upside potential reward to the producer, who in turn may have signed much of it away to a distributor, such as a Hollywood studio, which will always be in the best position to accept risk, as it can reduce risk through its interest in a diversified portfolio of projects.

Adequate accounting information is a critical factor in permitting efficient management of an enterprise on a global scale. Elliott (1992) considers the ways in which accounting may have to change in response to the new managerial problems encountered in the information age. In the case of film and television, this will require a re-examination of some of the fundamentals of accounting. For example, how useful is an accounting system that focuses on tangible assets—such as buildings, cameras, and film stock—when creative personnel and established contacts or inventories of cultural products themselves are the firm's real assets?

Similarly, in valuing these assets, rather than placing an emphasis on costs, which is the production side, it may be necessary to work out how the value created, on the customer side, can be brought into the picture. If producers are to focus outward on the consumers, then the accounting systems of these firms must be concerned with measuring the values created for firms. However, given the uncertainty and risk associated with the reception of film and television programmes, it is very difficult to obtain realistic estimates of the present value of the stream of future earnings.

Further, as Elliott (1992: 70) suggests, accounting systems must be developed to 'provide real time dials on the business rather than waiting for events to occur before recording them, thus providing only a retrospective look at the enterprise'. The feature film industry provides an interesting example of how this futuristic type of accounting system has already been implemented, with the use of daily accounting and production reports an industry norm. Leiterman describes current Canadian practice in Hehner (1987: 54–5).

Cost allocation is an important issue. Executives manage costs by overseeing activities rather than products. The pooling of costs by activities provides information that can help managers better to plan and control costs throughout the chain of business functions, from new product development to production. If a firm produces one product, all costs are applied to that product and accuracy of cost allocation is less of an issue. If there is only one process, it is usually not difficult to apply costs to diverse products according to the resources used in that single process. When there are many products and many activities, activity-based accounting may prove the best way to develop management accounting information.

### 10.2.12. If producers can never find movie project financing, how come so many movies get made?

Choice of a company's financing mix depends on taxes, risk, and asset type (Myers, 1983). As the debt:equity ratio is increased, the tax savings from interest deductibility become larger but the risk of financial distress (including the possibility of bankruptcy) and associated costs also increases. The optimal capital structure thus depends upon a trade-off between these two factors, and will vary with the risk of the company and the nature of its assets. Risk, in terms of the volatility of net income, is important because the greater the volatility, the lower the debt:equity ratio at which the possibility exists that the firm will be unable to meet interest obligations.

The nature of assets is relevant because some assets pass through bankruptcy largely unscathed (e.g. the real estate associated with a studio) while other assets, notably intangible assets such as human capital and technology, linked to the health of the firm as a going concern, are greatly diminished. Obviously intangible assets cannot provide good collateral for debt. The optimal capital structure will thus differ between firms depending on risk and asset type. Cable companies have relatively stable revenues while their assets are mainly in the form of physical plant. This suggests that a relatively high debt:equity ratio is appropriate. On the other hand, a small feature film producer is faced with highly variable revenues that depend on the box office for the firm's latest release, while the firm's assets are primarily the knowledge, abilities, and connections of the producer. This makes it desirable, whenever possible, to use equity financing. We note that recently several television/film production companies, including Alliance and Atlantis in Canada, have raised equity through initial public offerings.

Investing in a film or television programme is very risky. Finance theory distinguishes between two types of risk, systematic risk and unsystematic risk. The capital asset pricing model (CAPM) holds that the relevant risk of a security or a project is the systematic risk which measures the market-related risk that cannot be diversified away (Sharpe, 1964). This is indeed relevant for widely held public companies, where it is reasonable to suppose that shareholders are diversified. However, small film and television producers are typically closely held private companies where the owners have virtually all their eggs in one basket. For such owners the total risk, which also includes the unsystematic risk that is unique to the particular firm, is relevant. The unsystematic risk is particularly great if the firm is small (relative to the size of a typical industry project) and can thus handle only one project at a time, because there is then no portfolio of products or projects to partially diversify away risk. This means that feature film production, which normally involves a larger budget than television programme production, is especially high-risk.

Small producers usually seek funds on a project-by-project basis. Investing in an individual film is not often attractive for investors. Even insiders find it notoriously difficult to predict the commercial success of a given film. Furthermore, little (if any) collateral is typically available. On the other hand, large producers, notably the Hollywood studios, with their portfolio of films, can use the profits from past successes to finance new films. In addition, when external funds are required they can rely on their company reputation and collateral to attract financiers (see London Economics, 1992).

Closely held, usually small, producers are thus at a competitive disadvantage when compared with large, widely held US-style studios. Even Goldcrest, producer of hits like *Chariots of Fire* and *Gandhi*, went out of business after a short string of failures. In the words of Robert Evans (producer of *Chinatown*), as quoted by Litwak (1986), 'It only goes round once. It is like a parachute jump. If it doesn't open you are dead.'

### 10.2.13. *What other strategies are used to reduce risk?*

Prindle (1993) regards vertical integration as probably the most important risk-reducing strategy in the industry. As we have seen in Chapter 5, the Hollywood majors' distribution and, where permitted, exhibition activities have given them preferential access to cinemas. Vertical and horizontal integration to form media conglomerates has provided preferential access to other windows (e.g. Disney's formation of the Disney Channel, a channel carried on US cable TV) and other media (e.g. Time Warner produces and distributes not only films but also magazines, records, and books, and owns cable television franchises).

Co-productions reduce risk. As we saw in Chapter 9, they permit pooling of resources and improved access to foreign markets. For a given total budget, co-productions permit a producer to be involved in more projects, thus reducing risk through a greater portfolio effect. Pre-sale agreements with broadcasters, cable channels, and home video distributors also serve to get funds up-front.

## 10.4. CONCLUSION AND SUMMARY

In this chapter we have examined some aspects of the structure and management of the organizations which compete in the international film and television programme markets. Two crucial issues have been addressed: the structure and management of an organization that requires both creative and business skills to function effectively, and the extraordinary degree of uncertainty about consumer demand, and strategies for handling the resulting risk.

We briefly discussed each of these issues and then illustrated how they account for many of the intriguing issues managers face in these industries. To do this, we explored some of the principles of general management and organizational analysis, marketing and distribution, new product development, accounting and management information systems, and finance that explain the peculiarities of these industries. As film and television programmes typically have short lifecycles, it is the development of a stream of new films and/or programmes achieving critical and market acclaim that distinguishes successful producers. The new product development process and associated marketing strategies for managing creativity and handling uncertainty are of paramount importance in this environment.

# New Media and New Markets

New media will change television and film as we know it. Digitization brings with it the promise of changes as fundamental as those brought about by the development of the printing press five centuries ago or the introduction of broadcasting earlier this century. Digitization makes it possible for text, audio, and image data to be processed uniformly, thus making production, editing, reproduction and information retrieval much easier. Moreover, once a desired level of information quality is chosen it can be maintained, regardless of how many times information is retransmitted through time and space. In this chapter we examine how the new media can be expected to change the media environment, and the implications for the operations of the cultural industries, regulation and trade. Our discussion is based on Finn, Hoskins, McFadyen and Taylor (1996).

The new media environment is bringing conventional media firms, intent on capturing cyberspace as another window in their distribution system, together with a cast of new media creators and activists intent on creating virtual communities where people connect to each other, instead of just retrieving or receiving information. In media terms, whereas previous narrow-band technology led to mass media with a select few broadcasting, with networked broad-band capability we are moving towards the capability for the masses of narrowcasting.

Such a development would be a major advance on what is currently termed narrowcasting, that is, the distribution of speciality or niche channels. New media interfaces are being developed which move seamlessly between media that you steer (interactive) and media that steer you (passive). The result is an overall experience that combines many of the traits of computer networks and broadcasting. This convergence is what *Wired* (Mar. 1997, pp. 12–23) calls 'push media—content is pushed to you in contrast to the invitational pull you make when you click on the Web'. Although the Wall Street Journal may have 'trumpeted the arrival of push media by declaring that the Internet "has been in search of a viable business model. Now it has found one: television"', this new experience is not television. *Wired* observes:

the new networked media do borrow ideas from television, but the new media landscape will look nothing like television as we know it. And indeed it will transform television in the process. The promise of push–pull media is to marry the programmed experience of television with two key yearnings: navigating information and experience, and connecting to other people. With networked media you get TV's high production values along with the intense communal experience of watching something together—virtual communities. You also get the ability to address small self-organizing audiences that broadcast could never afford to find. And you get well-crafted stories seamlessly integrated into other media, such as online conversations. This heightened ability to extract meaning, experience, or community—rare with content pushed by broadcast—is almost the rule with content pushed on a network.

From an audiovisual industry perspective the key environmental factors can be broken down into technological and behavioural (see *TBI Yearbook 95*, pp. 373–4). The key technological changes are the development of broad-band switching equipment; the spread of optical fibre backbone for information networks; new higher-powered satellite transponder capabilities; the falling cost of digital storage and processing capacity (according to Moore's Law, these costs will continue to fall by 50 per cent every eighteen months); and the development of digital video imaging and compression technologies. Key behavioural changes which are important include familiarity with the use of keyboards, remote controls and joysticks for interacting with computers, television and game machines; acceptance of telecommunication beyond voice telephony because of experience with fax, e-mail, and the World Wide Web as well as familiarity with the greater control over one's media experience which comes from paying directly for video rentals, pay-TV channels, and pay-per-view. It is this broad set of technological and social changes that are driving the evolution of new media products.

Historically, new media have evolved gradually—from print to film to television. Recently technological change has rapidly accelerated this evolution. The driving force has been digitization, which has made it possible to reduce analogue text, sound, and images to digital information that can be transported by a common delivery system. This is what is behind the process of convergence—the merging of the communications, broadcasting, and computer industries (or, as George Gilder would have it, the collapsing of the telecommunications and broadcasting industries into the computer industry).

There are two distinct types of new media, one involving the communications infrastructure, the other involving the creative infrastructure. In the first type, existing media products are encoded/stored or distributed in novel ways. Television programmes, instead of being distributed by terrestrial broadcasters, may be distributed by cable, satellite, video cassette, CD-ROM, or DVD. The second type involves distinctive innovations in the nature of the communication medium itself. For example, feature films, instead of following a conventional unilinear plot sequence, may involve moviegoers in an interactive experience where their decisions affect the evolution of the story. (However, early evidence suggests people that value the structure of traditional storytelling.) Television programming may acquire computer game-like characteristics.

There is plenty of talk of the 500-channel television universe, and it is certainly easy to start up new low-cost services. The issue, though, is how are such offerings to be made commercially viable. For pay-per-view channels the market test is a direct one: revenues are proportional to the number of households signing on. Audience size is clearly also critical for advertiser-supported services and subscription services. If conventional terrestrial broadcasters are to remain viable they will need to continue to attract large numbers of viewers to their standardized, universal offerings. On the other hand, if the proponents of individualized 'Me TV' are correct, personalized sets of programme offerings may in future be constructed for viewers by intelligent agents built into electronic television guides. Niche channels directed at narrow audience segments would become more viable, by aggregating demand across space (international markets) and time. The ultimate limiting factor is the amount of time and money that consumers are willing to devote to (in this case) television-like viewing.

Convergence and disintermediation (the elimination of those distributors and retailers who currently bridge the gap between content producers and consumers) do not just bring once discrete cultural industries together. The digital media have developed from defence and computer industry innovation. Policies developed around the cultural industries as conventionally conceived (radio, television, cable, or film) can't deal effectively with the new digital entrants from the computer industry. Programmers are not just building tools any more: many software and computer game developers are pursuing digital media as a new art form. They are exerting a growing influence on the reinvention of the media sector.

In this chapter we do not intend to discuss specific media, technologies, or technological standards and assess which are likely to triumph. Predictions of this sort might be outdated even before publication date. Instead we focus on some effects of technological developments which we can confidently predict will occur regardless of the success or failure of specific media, technologies, or technological standards. These effects are the elimination of the significance of geographical distance, the continual reduction of the costs of information services over time, the ascent of access and marginalization of monopoly, the ongoing search for the killer application, the favouring of both the individual and the global, and the replacement of government diktat by consumer sovereignty. After discussing these effects, we then draw the implications for the operations of the cultural industries, regulation, censorship, employment, and trade.

## 11.1. EFFECTS OF TECHNOLOGICAL DEVELOPMENTS

### *11.1.1. Digitization destroys distance*

It is clear that distance will become increasingly irrelevant as the digital revolution drives down the cost of all forms of communication and information transmission. Information stored on the other side of the world has become just as accessible as information stored next door. As a consequence, many of the cost factors which traditionally favoured the clustering of production activities, and the close proximity of production to the market, will be weakened. There will still be a place, albeit a lesser place, for Hollywood, with its face-to-face contact for players from all segments of the industry.

### *11.1.2. The continual reduction in the costs of information services*

Transaction costs are those costs arising from searching for someone with whom to do business, of reaching an agreement about the price and other conditions of the exchange, and of ensuring that the terms of the agreement are fulfilled. The real cost of acquiring, processing, storing, and transmitting digital information will continue to decline for the foreseeable future with the improvement in compression technologies and the expansion of band-width. With network penetration continuing to climb, increasing competition will ensure the benefits are passed on in the form of lower prices. This will reduce the size of transaction costs relative to other costs in the feature film and television business as well as business in general.

### *11.1.3. The ascent of access and the marginalization of monopoly*

Whereas governments, rights associations, and industry participants have historically been able to regulate access or maintain geographical market monopolies, the power to do so will disappear with the development of alternative avenues of access to information services. Of course, there will continue to be areas where the high infrastructure costs for new entrants will limit competition during a transition period, but this will only apply in areas where the ultimate demand is limited. Monopolies will be limited to low income and less educated neighbourhoods.

### *11.1.4. The search for the killer basket*

While there is some evidence that television is losing some of its audience to the World Wide Web, there is a deep-seated suspicion that entertainment products alone will never become the so-called 'killer app'—a shorthand borrowed from the computer industry to describe an application that drives up computer penetration. A myopic search for the killer app may cause decision-makers to dismiss technologies and applications that may not support the entire infrastructure on their own. But entertainment may prove to be a valuable component of a killer basket of online goods and services, in combination with electronic commerce, banking, education, telephony, and home security, among others. The Price Waterhouse *1997 Technology Forecast*, for example, estimates that electronic commerce will grow from $183 million on the Internet and $679 million on corporate intranets in 1996 to $12 billion on the Internet and $32 billion on intranets by the year 2000 (*Globe and Mail*, 26 Feb. 1997, p. B9).

### 11.1.5. *The favouring of the individual and the global*

In many ways the conventional and new media are competing to define two terms common to both their vocabularies—the individual and global. Both claim to offer the individual considerable sovereignty and both see the global community as a shared space. But for the new media model the shared culture is negotiated collectively from within; for conventional media the shared culture is imposed from without. The entertainment industry sees itself, and is frequently seen by its critics, as the creator of a global culture—made up of images, sounds, and symbols—that are shared by individual consumers. A wired world—of which the Internet may prove to be only a prototype—favours the individual and the global over the national and the local.

### 11.1.6. *The replacement of government diktat by consumer sovereignty*

What is actually going to happen in areas such as multipoint distribution services (wireless cable), digital compression, interactive television, or technology standards, such as MPEG, encryption, and Java? It is important to realize that no one has the answer—including civil servants and members of quasi-judicial regulatory bodies such as the Australian Broadcasting Authority. Government regulators should resist the urge to pick winners and losers. Major corporations have made large investments in field trials of video-on-demand to try to find out some of the answers on technology and consumer preferences. More recently, strategic focus has shifted to mergers and alliances across borders of industries and nations. These cross-holdings provide a way for corporations to hedge their bets, by having a stake in many alternatives, in an uncertain environment where a few big wins and many losses are likely to occur.

## 11.2. IMPLICATIONS FOR THE CULTURAL INDUSTRIES

The technological developments we have described have foreseeable implications for traditional cultural industries in the areas of production, marketing, and distribution.

### 11.2.1. Production

As new digital technologies have replaced traditional analogue methods of sound and visual recording and editing, both the capital cost of equipment and the number of technicians needed to operate the equipment have begun to decline. Basement-level desktop audio and video are rapidly approaching the quality once only achieved in costly-to-rent professional recording studios and sound stages. There will be a significant reduction in what are referred to as below-the-line costs, namely the facility and technical production costs, relative to the above-the-line creative costs of stars, scripts, and directors. The most important implications are:

1. A weakening of the traditional studios and production centres which have made major investments in fixed production facilities and a relative strengthening of the power of established creativity suppliers (agents, stars, independent producers).
2. A weakening of the power of the production unions as scenes synthetically created by computer are able to replace those built by carpenters, decorators, electricians, and other tradesmen, and production switched to less restrictive labour environments.
3. A sharp increase in the value of existing stocks of sources of creativity. Intellectual property is the real property of the information economy. Consequences include increased numbers of sequels and remakes of stories which have been successful in other cultures and languages. There may be even higher payments to stars, although the possibilities of computer-generated 'virtual actors' and the growing use of special effects as the real stars (as in *Twister* and *Volcano*) provide a counterbalance.
4. A lowering of barriers to entry. Further developments in video cameras and desktop video suggest that technology-based barriers to entry for production are in the process of disappearing. Thus the number of industry participants can be expected to explode.

### 11.2.2. Marketing

The weakening of the traditional advertising-supported mass media and the advent of new forms of information distribution, expected to follow from falling transaction costs, will result in a reduction in media placement costs relative to creative costs. The most important implication is an increase in the power of established communication and entertainment brands or sources with a distinctive identity or brand equity (such as Disney, the BBC, CNN, and CityTV in Toronto) relative to participants who lack any strong identity (for examples, ITV in the UK, MCA which is changing to Universal, and the CTV private English-language network in Canada).

### 11.2.3. Distribution

1. A widespread network will exist for two-way high speed digital communication to the home. While we cannot be sure there will be competition between such networks in every geographical market, each market will be contested. Any significant exploitation of monopoly power in a market will provide the necessary incentive for competitive developments to thwart the exploitation.

2. Competition will increase sharply as the media industries move from regional geographical monopolies (cable systems) or oligopolies (city newspapers, cinema exhibition) towards highly competitive market structures, where the only market boundaries are created by language, culture, and lifestyle interests.

3. A sharp increase can be expected in the value of existing libraries of programmes, especially those which can be supplied to services targeting narrow market niches.

### 11.2.4. Transactions

The substantial drop in transaction costs between buyers and sellers who are geographically separated will lead to:

1. A movement away from production centralized near important creative centres or distribution centres such as Hollywood and London, to more widely scattered locations providing unique character or creative convenience, such as British Columbia or Queensland.

2. A potential for significant disintermediation as producers and consumers are more able economically to conduct transactions directly without the intervening role of distributors and exhibitors. Independent film distribution on the Internet is one possibility. Consumers with strong preferences will be able to seek out the specific products or services they wish to acquire and complete a low-cost economic transaction, reducing the power of the traditional hierarchical distribution channel. However, new forms of intermediary are likely to develop to assist in other aspects of the exchange process. These are likely to include search agents, payment agents, and copyright collection agents. New forms of retailers may develop, in competition with traditional exhibitors, to satisfy preferences for social consumption of entertainment programmes, rather than individualized

consumption. Such retailers may develop out of existing bars, libraries, and restaurants, and may be foreshadowed in the recent enthusiasm for cybercafés.

## 11.3. IMPLICATIONS FOR REGULATION

In the emerging competitive environment, the consumer is the common decision-point and should be free to choose from the widest range of delivery systems. Bureaucrats and regulators have got into hot water by placing big bets on specific technologies. An example is the EU's failed attempt to impose (at a public cost of 4 billion ECU) a specific High Definition Standard. Another is the failure of Japan's grand twenty-year plan to build the Information Network System, an all-encompassing national communications grid.

Alvin Toffler argues that the new media are 'culture busters'. Language translation technologies (already in place in Japan) will allow media products to cross linguistic market borders.

That affects the very deepest fundamentals of culture. It allows us to take a bit from here and a bit from there and configure a new personality and culture that is totally unique to the established perceptions of our cultures today. You will still have an Australian culture, or a Malaysian culture or whatever, but it will be a very different Australian culture to what you have now. (cited in Plunkett, 1994: 36)

Governments will not be able to regulate availability or access to particular forms of content. Restrictions on access or content quotas (TV and radio) will become unenforceable as consumers become free to switch to channels which can deliver equivalent types of content without being subject to such restrictions. Governments can influence consumption through support for access for those who might otherwise be unable to obtain it. The Japanese government report on *The Convergence of Communications and Broadcasting toward the 21st Century* (*New Breeze*, 1996: 24) recommends that, in response to information disparities, 'we must launch education programs on how to operate information equipment'. With low-cost Internet appliances soon to become available, this approach has merit. Governments can also influence the availability of domestic content through direct support for its production. If we accept the premiss of convergence—that digital technology brings together once distinct industries and technologies—what are the prospects for a policy that places cultural obligations on some players and not on others?

Many countries have traditionally linked content and carriage regulation. Licensed carriers are obligated to meet certain content criteria through original production or acquisition, but benefit from government incentives to nurture the production of indigenous content. Convergence creates havoc for such a regime. Taking Canada as a case study, consider the recent policy statement of the CRTC (the Canadian broadcasting regulatory agency):

It is the Commission's recommendation . . . that the Broadcasting Act be amended, perhaps by way of suitable changes to the definition of 'program,' so as to exclude . . . other services that, while they likely fall within the definition of broadcasting, will not foreseeably contribute materially to the achievement of the Broadcasting Act's objectives. (CRTC, 1995: 30)

Canada's Broadcasting Act treats media as a closed system that can be regulated through the maintenance of a 'cultural border'. But the Internet, a network designed to withstand a nuclear blast, does not respect such borders. The tension between the closed system assumed by the Broadcasting Act and a ubiquitous and open digital network is self-evident. The lesson of the Internet has been that it is not a good idea to assume that there are necessarily things that it will or will not do. The lesson needs to be applied more broadly to all the industrial sectors that are involved in media convergence. The process of determining at this early stage which services might or might not 'contribute materially' to the Act's objectives is sheer folly. The malleability of digital content, and its apparent platform agnosticism calls out for deregulation. If content merits special government attention because it is 'cultural glue' that holds the country together, then incentives should be directed at production and consumption of such content, not at a delivery mechanism. The process of new media evolution is so fluid and rapid that regulators will be forever caught off-guard and off-base.

## 11.4. IMPLICATIONS FOR CENSORSHIP

A US federal court has come out with a strong opinion rejecting the basic tenets of the Communications Decency Act on free-speech grounds. Other countries should take heed. Although the decision should be made on principle, there are also practical grounds for avoiding attempts at censorship. They will not work. The Internet was designed to withstand war conditions by routing information through alternative pathways should direct routes be blocked. This design feature ensures the failure in practice of any censorship regime.

Even the censorship exercised by regulators and cable services, in terms of determining which channels will be offered, can be expected to disappear soon: 'The control over access to information that a cable operator exercises will come to be regarded in 10, 15, 20 years time, as anachronistic by both information providers and consumers. There is no place for the meddling middle man in the new communications era.' (*TBI Yearbook 95*, p. 373.)

## 11.5. IMPLICATIONS FOR EMPLOYMENT

Technological changes always bring with them the fear of displacement of workers by machines. Digitization and new media, like technological innovations in the past, will both destroy millions of jobs and create millions of new jobs. What individual countries have to be concerned about is the extent to which the new jobs are created at home. Subsidies to domestic-content creators may protect some jobs. But the major concern is that government barriers that merely delay the development of the necessary information infrastructure will severely limit job creation, not only in new media-related areas but economy-wide. Any country that does not develop an information highway will no longer be part of the global political and trading arena. The cost to countries that attempt to continue regulatory protection of cable and telecommunication monopolists may be very high.

## 11.6. IMPLICATIONS FOR TRADE

In this section we examine the implications of media developments for US dominance of trade and for international trade disputes.

### 11.6.1. *Implications for US dominance*

How will the emergence of the new media affect US dominance of trade in television and film? This question can be approached by re-examining, in the context of trade, the implications (identified earlier in this chapter) for the cultural industries.

Factors tending to lessen US dominance:

1. The significant reduction in below-the-line costs relative to the above-the-line creative costs will lessen the importance of the traditional studios and production centres with their major investments in fixed production facilities.
2. The substantial drop in transaction costs between buyers and sellers who are geographically separated will lead to a movement away from production centralized near important creative centres or distribution centres such as Hollywood to more widely scattered locations providing unique character or creative convenience.
3. Consumers with strong preferences will be able to seek out the specific products or services they wish to acquire and complete a low-cost economic transaction, reducing the power of the traditional hierarchical distribution channel associated with the Hollywood majors.

4. Further developments in video cameras and desktop video suggest that technology-based barriers to entry are in the process of disappearing. The number of industry participants can be expected to explode, thus weakening the relative importance of the major players.

Factors tending to maintain US dominance:

1. Intellectual property is the 'real property' of the information economy, and the increase in the value of existing stocks of sources of creativity that can be expected will benefit the Hollywood majors with their extensive software libraries. The majors have the marketing muscle to build consumer awareness of television programmes and feature films under their control. The new media create additional links in the chain of exhibition windows, through which the majors are able to exploit these rights. A longer chain of exhibition windows coupled with price discrimination between windows (i.e. less valued venues being priced lower; e.g. video rental is less costly than theatre admission) will permit the majors fully to extract the economic value of their products.
2. Hollywood is the major centre of established creative suppliers—agents, stars, independent producers—and can be expected to benefit from the increase in above-the-line costs relative to below-the-line costs.

Factors that are neutral or indeterminate in terms of US dominance:

1. The weakening of the traditional advertising supported mass media and the advent of new forms of information distribution will result in a reduction in media placement costs relative to the creative costs. The most important implication is an increase in the power of established communication and entertainment brands or sources with a distinctive identity or brand equity relative to participants who lack any strong identity. Some of those that benefit, such as Disney and CNN, will be American, but so will non-US entities such as the BBC and CityTV in Toronto. Similarly, likely losers include a studio like MCA (which, having identified this problem, has changed its name to Universal) or a network like CTV, the private English-language network in Canada.
2. The expected increase in the value of existing libraries of programmes which can be supplied to services targeting narrow market niches can be expected to benefit suppliers such as Disney, in the US, and Anglia, the ITV company in the UK that has established a reputation for natural history programming.

In weighing these effects we conclude that the forces leading to decentralization of production and distribution are likely to diminish the US advantage somewhat, but that Hollywood will still be in a strong position as the leading concentration of creative talent.

## 11.6.2. *Implications for international trade disputes*

As we saw in Chapter 1, trade in cultural products has always been particularly sensitive. Washington has served notice that it intends to revisit
the cultural provisions of GATT under the new World Trade Organization
(WTO). One of the most daunting challenges for the WTO will be managing global trade in a digital age: 'When you go through customs you
declare your atoms, not your bits' (Negroponte, 1995: 4). The issue is
further complicated when those bits carry cultural significance. Border controls on bits are bound to be problematic.

Problems of copyright and piracy are likely to increase. As Yaqub (1996)
observes:

First, due to the nature of digital technology, 'generational loss' (the physical dete-
rioration that occurs with each progressive copy when copies are made in an analog
medium) is a thing of the past; endless numbers of perfect copies can be made. Secondly, the accessibility of the global network makes it possible to distribute copies
on a global scale, without the need for traditional (hard-to establish) underground
distribution channels or interference from customs.

However, activity on global networks will in fact also be more readily mon-
itored—and thus disputes will be better publicized.

We can only expect international trade disputes in this area to grow in
complexity and frequency.

### 11.7. CONCLUSION

The new forms of content and connectivity ushered in by digitization are
in their infancy. Video-on-demand trials have failed to live up to their
advance billing, and interactive movies on CD-ROM have not yet found
wide audiences among either movie buffs or video game enthusiasts. Many
of these experiments were easily dismissed in years past—as are many
experimental current uses of Web-based technologies, including desktop
video, real-time bit stream audio and video, and the emerging GUI Virtual
Worlds. What many critics have failed fully to appreciate is that we are
watching rehearsals.

The analog–digital transformation parallels an early transformation from
oral to print cultures: 'speechasencodedvisuallyinwritingisnotspeechanylonger'
(McLuhan, 1969: 24). By extension, a digitized film is no longer a film,
a digitized book is no longer a book, digital television content is no longer
TV. Instead, the content from once discrete industries are fodder for nothing
less than a new digital orality in which conventional assumptions about
how media are produced and used are suspect. There has been a rush to
're-purpose' film, television, and audio content for distribution on the
much-trumpeted Information Superhighway. If we accept McLuhan's for-

mulations, and acknowledge that a generation raised on video games demands to interact with content differently from their parents, there will be both technological and market pressures to exploit the unique benefits of digital media.

In this chapter we have not attempted to predict which specific technologies or standards will triumph. Instead we have identified some effects of new media development which can be expected to occur regardless. These effects are the elimination of the significance of geographical distance, the continual reduction of the costs of information services over time, the ascent of access and marginalization of monopoly, the ongoing search for the 'killer basket' of applications, the favouring of both the individual and the global, and the replacement of government diktat by consumer sovereignty. The implications include:

1. The traditional cultural industries can expect a strengthening of the power of established creativity suppliers relative to traditional studios, a sharp increase in the value of existing stocks of sources of creativity, a lowering of barriers to entry, an increase in the value of established communication and entertainment brands, a move away from centralized production centres, and an increased competition in distribution and a reduction in the strength of the traditional hierarchical distribution channel.
2. As public policy is developed and adapted to the emerging digital environment, the unprecedented malleability (and nonlinearity) of digital content is ignored at peril. The process of new media evolution is so fluid and rapid that regulation is not appropriate.
3. The forces leading to decentralization of production and distribution are likely to diminish the US advantage somewhat, but Hollywood will still be in a strong position as the leading concentration of creative talent.

# References

ACHESON, K., and MAULE, C. (1990). 'Canadian Content Rules: A Time for Reconsideration', *Canadian Public Policy*, 16(3): 284–97.
——(1996). *International Agreements and the Cultural Industries*. Ottawa: Centre for Trade Policy and Law.
AKSOY, A., and ROBINS, K. (1992). 'Hollywood for the 21st Century: Global Competition for Critical Mass in Image Markets', *Cambridge Journal of Economics*, 16: 1–22.
ALVARADO, M. (1989). *Global Video*. London: BRU/UNESCO/John Libbey.
AUSTIN, B. A. (1989). *Immediate Seating: a Look at Movie Audiences*. Belmont, Calif.: Wadsworth.
BAKER, W., and FAULKNER, R. (1991). 'Role as Resource in the Hollywood Film Industry', *American Journal of Sociology*, 97 (Sept.): 279–309.
BARWISE, P., and EHRENBERG, A. (1988). *Television and Its Audience*, London: Sage.
BERWANGER, D. (1987). *Television in the Third World: New Technology and Social Change*. Bonn: Friedrich-Ebert-Stiftung.
BIRD, R., BUCOVETSKY, M., and YATCHEW, A. (1981). *Tax Incentives for the Canadian Film Industry*. Toronto: Institute for Policy Analysis, University of Toronto.
BLUMLER, J., and HOFFMAN-RIEM, W. (1992). 'New Roles for Public Television in Western Europe: Challenges and Prospects', *Journal of Communication*, 42(1): 20–35.
BOARDMAN, A., and VINING, A. (1996). 'Public Service Broadcasting in Canada', *Journal of Media Economics*, 9(1): 47–62.
BODDY, W. (1994). 'U.S. Television Abroad: Market Power and National Introspection', *Quarterly Review of Film and Video*, 15(2): 45–55.
BOYD, D. (1985). 'VCRs in Developing Countries: An Arab Case Study', *Media Development*, 32(1): 5–7.
BOYD-BARRETT, O. (1977). 'Media Imperialism: Toward an International Framework for the Analysis of Media Systems', in J. Curran et al. (eds.), *Mass Communication and Society*. London: Arnold.
BOYLE, H. (1977). 'Testimony Before the House of Commons Standing Committee on Broadcasting, Films and Assistance to the Arts', 22 Mar., Ottawa.
BROWN, A. (1996). 'Economics, Public Service Broadcasting and Social Values', *Journal of Media Economics*, 9(1): 3–16.
BROWN, C. (ed.) (1995). *Co-production International 1995*. London: 21st Century Business Publications, FT Media and Telecoms.
BTCE (1991). *Economic Aspects of Broadcast Regulation*. Bureau of Transport and Communications Economics, Report 71. Canberra: Commonwealth of Australia, Australian Government Publishing Service.

Canada, Task Force on Film Distribution, Exhibition and Marketing (1983). *Task Force Report*. Ottawa.

Canada, Film Industry Task Force (1985). *Canadian Cinema: A Solid Base*. Ottawa.

Canada, Task Force on Broadcasting Policy (1986). *Report*. Ottawa: Minister of Supply and Services.

CHAPMAN, G. (1987). 'Towards a Geography of the Tube: TV Flows in Western Europe', *Intermedia* (Jan.): 10–21.

CHRISTOPHERSON, S., and STORPER, M. (1986). 'The City as Studio; The World as Back Lot: The Impact of Vertical Disintegration on the Location of the Motion Picture Industry', *Environment and Planning D: Society and Space*, 4: 305–20.

————(1989). 'The Effects of Flexible Specialization in Industrial Politics and the Labour Market: The Motion Picture Industry', *Industrial and Labor Relations Review*, 42(3): 331–47.

COLLINS, R. (1988). *Culture, Communications and National Identity: The Case of Canadian Television*. Toronto: University of Toronto Press.

————(1989). 'The Language of Advantage: Satellite Television in Western Europe', *Media, Culture and Society*, 11: 351–71.

————GARNHAM, N., and LOCKSLEY, G. (1986). *The Economics of Television: The UK Case*. London: Sage.

CONLOGUE, R. (1993). 'Taking a Stand for the Cinematic National Soul', *Globe and Mail* (Toronto) (21 Dec.): A12.

CONTRACTOR, F., and LORANGE, P. (1988). 'Competition vs. Cooperation: A Benefit/Cost Framework for Choosing Between Fully-Owned Investments and Co-operative Relationships', *Management International Review*, special issue on Co-operative Issues in International Business, 28: 5–18.

COOPER, R. (1980). *Project New Prod: What Makes a New Product a Winner?* Montreal: Centre Québecois d'Innovation Industrielle.

————and KLEINSCHMIDT, E. (1990). *New Products: The Key Factors in Success*. Chicago: American Marketing Association.

COX, R. (1987). 'Pitfalls of Co-production', *Playback* (Toronto) (28 June): 40.

CRTC (1995). *Competition and Culture on Canada's Information Highway: Managing the Realities of Transition*. Ottawa: Supply and Services Canada.

CRYAN, J., JOHNSON, D., CRANE, J., and CAMMARATA, A. (1988). 'Strategies for the International Production and Distribution of Feature Films in 1990s', *Loyola Entertainment Law Journal*, 8: 1–24.

CUNNINGHAM, S., and JACKA, E. (1996). *Australian Television and International Mediascapes*. Melbourne: Cambridge University Press.

CVAR, M. (1996). 'Case Studies in Global Competition: Patterns of Success and Failure', in M. Porter (ed.), *Competition in Global Industries*. Boston: Harvard Business School Press, 483–516.

DALY, D. (1980). *A Comparison of Exhibition and Distribution Patterns in Three Recent Feature Motion Pictures*. New York: Arno Press.

DE GRAZIA, V. (1989). 'Mass Culture and Sovereignty: The American Challenge to European Cinemas, 1920–1960', *Journal of Modern History*, 61 (Mar.): 53–87.

DIAMOND, H. (1989). 'Lights, Camera . . . Research!' *Marketing News*, 23 (11 Sept.): 10–11.

DONAHUE, S. (1987). *American Film Distribution: The Changing Marketplace*. Ann Arbor, Mich.: UMI Research Press.

*Economist, The* (1986). London, 10 May.

ELLIOTT, R. (1992). 'The Third Wave Breaks on the Shores of Accounting', *Accounting Horizons*, 6 (June): 61–85.

ELLIS, D. (1992). *Split Screen: Home Entertainment and the New Technologies*. Toronto: Friends of Canadian Broadcasting.

FARLEY, J. (1986). 'Are There Truly International Products—and Prime Prospects for Them?' *Journal of Advertising Research* (Oct./Nov.): 17–20.

FINLER, J. (1992). *The Hollywood Story*. London: Mandarin.

FINN, A., HOSKINS, C., and McFADYEN, S. (1996). 'Telefilm Canada Investment in Feature Films: Empirical Foundations for Public Policy', *Canadian Public Policy*, 12(2): 151–61.

————and TAYLOR, P. (1996). 'Policy Directions for the New Media Environment', *Policy Options*, 17(8): 40–3.

————(1994). 'Marketing, Management And Competitive Strategy in the Cultural Industries', *Canadian Journal of Communication*, 19: 523–50.

————(1995). 'Le Développement de nouveaux produits dans les industries culturelles', *Recherche et Applications en Marketing*, 10(4): 47–63.

FUHRMAN, C. (1989). *Publicity Stunt*. San Francisco, Calif.: Chronicle Books.

FULFORD, R. (1986). 'Blaming the Yanks', *Saturday Night* (Toronto).

GARNHAM, N., and LOCKSLEY, G. (1991). 'The Economics of Broadcasting', in J. Blumler and T. Nossiter (eds.), *Broadcasting in Transition*. New York: Oxford University Press.

GILDER, G. (1994). *Life After Television*, rev. edn. New York: Norton.

GITLIN, T. (1983). *Inside Prime Time*. New York: Pantheon.

GLOBERMAN, S. (1987). *Culture, Governments and Markets: Public Policy and the Cultural Industries*. Vancouver: Fraser Institute.

——and VINING, A. (1987). *Foreign Ownership and Canada's Feature Film Distribution Sector: An Economic Analysis*. Vancouver: Fraser Institute.

GOLDBERG, F. (1991). *Motion Picture: Marketing and Distribution*. Boston: Focal Press, Butterworth-Heinemann.

GRAHAM, A., and DAVIES, G. (1992). 'The Public Funding of Broadcasting', in T. Congdon et al., *Paying for Broadcasting: The Handbook*. London: Routledge, 167–221.

GUBACK, T. (1969). *The International Film Industry*. Bloomington: Indiana University Press.

——(1984). 'International Circulation of U.S. Theatrical Films and Television Programming', in G. Gerbner and M. Siefert (eds.), *World Communications: A Handbook*. New York: Longman, 153–63.

——(1985a). 'Government Financial Support to the Film Industry in the United States', in B. Austin (ed.), *Current Research in Film: Audiences, Economics and Law*, iii. Norwood, NJ: Ablex, 88–104.

——(1985b). 'Non-market Factors in the International Distribution of American Films', in B. Austin (ed.), *Current Research in Film: Audiences, Economics and Law*, ii. Norwood, NJ: Ablex, 111–26.

HEHNER, B. (ed.) (1987). *Making It: The Business of Film and Television Production in Canada*. Toronto: Academy of Canadian Cinema and Television.

HILL, J. (1994). 'The Future of European Cinema: The Economics and Culture of Pan-European Strategies', in J. Hill, M. McLoone, and P. Hainsworth (eds.),

*Border Crossing: Film in Ireland, Britain and Europe*. Belfast: Institute of Irish Studies.

HIRSCHMAN, E. (1983). 'Aesthetics, Ideologies and the Limits of the Marketing Concept', *Journal of Marketing*, **47** (summer): 45–55.

HISE, R., O'NEAL, L., MCNEAL, J., and PARASURAMAN, A. (1990). 'Marketing/R&D Interaction in New Product Development: Implications for New Product Success Rates', *Journal of Product Innovation Management*, 7: 142–55.

HOSKINS, C., FINN, A., and MCFADYEN, S. (1996). 'Television and Film in a Freer International Trade Environment: US Dominance and Canadian Responses', in E. McAnany and K. Wilkinson (eds.), *Mass Media and Free Trade: NAFTA and the Cultural Industries*. Austin: University of Texas Press.

HOSKINS, C., and MCFADYEN, S. (1985). 'The Whys and Wherefores of Television Broadcasting Regulations and Incentives', in C. Hoskins and S. McFadyen (eds.), *Canadian Broadcasting: The Challenge of Change*. Edmonton: University of Alberta, 15–22.

——— (1986). 'New Delivery Technologies and the Globalization of the Television Programming Industry: The Marketing of Indian Films and Television Programs in Canada', *Service Industries Journal* (Mar.): 90–103.

——— (1989). 'Television in the New Broadcasting Environment: Public Policy Lessons from the Canadian Experience', *European Journal of Communication*, 4: 173–89.

——— (1991a). 'International Marketing Strategies for a Cultural Service', *International Marketing Review*, 8(2): 40–52.

——— (1991b). 'The US Competitive Advantage in the Global Market: Is It Sustainable in the New Broadcast Environment?' *Canadian Journal of Communication*, 16(2): 207–24.

——— (1992). 'The Mandate, Structure and Financing of the CBC', *Canadian Public Policy*, 8(3): 275–89.

——— (1993). 'Canadian Participation in International Co-productions and Co-ventures in Television Programming', *Canadian Journal of Communication*, 18(2): 219–36.

——— (1995). 'Cost Savings through Restructuring of the CBC', Winner of the Federal Category of the 1994–5 Fraser Institute Economy in Government Competition.

——— (1996). 'The Mandate, Structure and Financing of the CBC', in H. Holmes and D. Taras (eds.), *Seeing Ourselves: Media Power and Policy in Canada*, 2nd edn. Toronto: Harcourt Brace, 285–301.

——— and FINN, A. (1997). 'A Comparison of the Motivation of Japanese and Canadian Participants in International Joint Ventures in Television and Film: The Role of Cultural Distance and Management Culture', in P. Beamish and J. Kelley (eds.), *Cooperative Strategies: Asian Perspectives*, San Francisco: New Lexington Press.

——— and JACKEL, A. (1995). 'Film and Television Co-production: Evidence from Canadian–European Experience', *European Journal of Communication*, 10(2): 221–43.

——— and MIRUS, R. (1988). 'Reason for the US Dominance of the International Trade in Television Programmes', *Media, Culture and Society*, 10: 499–515.

——— and ROZEBOOM, W. (1989). 'US Television Programs in the International Market: Unfair Pricing?' *Journal of Communication*, 39(2): 55–75.

INMAN, J., and WHEAT, R. (1992). 'Predicting Entertainment Event Sales Patterns: The Role of Marketability and Playability', paper presented at the 1992 TIMS Marketing Science Conference, London.

JANISCH, H. (1987). 'Canada: Culture or Commerce', *Intermedia*, 15(4/5): 42–3.

JENSEN, R., and MECKLING, W. (1976). 'Theory of the Firm: Managerial Behavior, Agency Costs and Ownership Structure', *Journal of Financial Economics*, 11: 305–60.

KESSLER, K. (1995). 'Protecting Free Trade in Audiovisual Entertainment: A Proposal for Counteracting the European Union's Trade Barriers to the US Entertainment Industry's Exports', *Law and Policy in International Business*, 26(2): 563–611.

KLAPRAT, C. (1985). 'The Star as Market Strategy: Bette Davis in Another Light', in T. Balio (ed.), *The American Film Industry*, rev. edn. Madison: University of Wisconsin Press.

KRIDER, R., and WEINBERG, C. (1992). 'A Dynamic Model of Competitive Innovation: Motion Picture Revenues Over Time', paper presented at the 1992 TIMS Marketing Science Conference, London.

LARSEN, P. (ed.) (1990). *Import/Export: International Flow of Television Fiction*. Paris: Unesco.

LEALAND, G. (1984). *American Television Programs on British Screens*. London: Broadcasting Research Unit.

LEE, C. (1980). *Media Imperialism Reconsidered: The Homogenizing of Television Culture*. Beverly Hills, Calif.: Sage.

LITMAN, B. R. (1983). 'Predicting Success of Theatrical Movies: An Empirical Study', *Journal of Popular Culture*, 16 (spring): 159–75.

LITWAK, M. (1986). *Reel Power*. New York: William Morrow.

London Economics (1992). *The Competitive Position of the European and US Film Industries*. Report for the Media Business School (an initiative of the MEDIA programme of the European Community, London).

McFADYEN, S., HOSKINS, C., and FINN, A. (1996). *Film and Television Co-production in Australia*. Canberra: Bureau of Transportation and Communication Economics.

McLUHAN, M. (1969). *Counterblast*. New York: Harcourt, Brace & World.

McQUEEN, D. (1983). 'Alternative Scenarios in Broadcasting', *Canadian Public Policy*, 9(2): 129–34.

Mandate Review Committee (1996). *Making Our Voices Heard: Canadian Broadcasting and Film for the 21st Century*. Ottawa: Minister of Supply and Services.

MARQUES DE MELO, J. (1988). 'Brazilian Television Fiction: Production and Export: Case Study of TV Globo', paper sponsored by UNESCO and presented at the Consultation of Experts on International Dissemination of TV Drama, Hilversum, Holland, 22–4 Feb.

——(1990). 'Brazilian Television Fiction', in P. Larsen (ed.), *Import/Export: International Flow of Television Fiction*. Reports and Papers on Mass Communication, No. 104. Paris: UNESCO.

——(1995). 'Development of the Audiovisual Industry in Brazil From Importer to Exporter of Television Programming', *Canadian Journal of Communication*, 20(3): 317–28.

MATTELART, A., DELACOURT, X., and MATTELART, M. (1984). *International Image Markets*. London: Comedia.

MAULE, C. (1989). 'The Nation State and Trade in Cultural Services', *Canadian Journal of Communication*, 14(2): 88–94.

Media Business School (Media Documentation Center (MEDOC)) (1995). 'What's Gone Wrong?' 24 May, Madrid.

MEISEL, J. (1986). 'Escaping Extinction: Cultural Defense of an Undefended Border', in D. Flaherty and W. McKercher (eds.), *Southern Exposure: Canadian Perspectives on the United States*. Toronto: McGraw-Hill Ryerson, 152–68.

MILLS, P. (1985). 'An International Audience', *Media, Culture and Society* (Oct.): 487–501.

MONTGOMERY-SCHELL, C. (1989). 'Producers Expanding Scope of Operations', *Playback* (Toronto) (27 Nov.): 33.

MYERS, S. (1983). 'The Search for Optimal Capital Structure', *Midland Corporate Finance Journal* (spring): 6–16.

NEGROPONTE, N. (1995). *Being Digital*. New York: Knopf.

*New Breeze* (1996). 8(3) (summer): 23–9. Tokyo: New ITV Association of Japan.

NOAM, E. (1993). 'Media Americanization, National Culture, and Forces of Integration', in E. Noam and J. Millonzi (eds.), *The International Market for Film and Television Programs*. Norwood, NJ: Ablex, 41–58.

NORDENSTRENG, K., and VARIS, T. (1974). *Television Traffic: One-Way Street? A Survey and Analysis of the International Flow of Television Programme Material*. Reports and papers on Mass Communication, No. 70. Paris: UNESCO.

NYLEN, D. W. (1990). *Marketing Decision-making Handbook*. Englewood Cliffs, NJ: Prentice-Hall.

O'DONNELL, P., and McDOUGAL, D. (1992). *Fatal Subtraction*. New York: Doubleday.

OHMAE, K. (1989). 'Managing in a Borderless World', *Harvard Business Review* (May–June 1989): 153–61.

OWEN, B., and WILDEMAN, S. (1992). *Video Economics*. Cambridge, Mass.: Harvard University Press.

PEACOCK, A. (chairman) (1986). *Report of the Committee on Financing the BBC*. London: HMSO.

PENDAKUR, M. (1982). 'Cultural Dependency in Canada's Feature Film Industry', in G. Kindem (ed.), *The American Film Industry*. Carbondale: Southern Illinois University Press, 351–60.

——(1990). *Canadian Dreams and American Control: The Political Economy of the Canadian Film Industry*. Detroit: Wayne State University Press.

PHAM, A., and WATSON, N. (1993). *The Film Marketing Handbook*, ed. J. Durie. Fundacion Cultural Media.

PLUNKETT, S. (1994). 'The Superhighway to a See-Through Society', *21C* (autumn): 36.

PORTER, M. (1986). 'Competition in Global Industries: A Conceptual Framework', in M. Porter (ed.), *Competition in Global Industries*. Boston: Harvard Business School Press, 15–60.

PORTMAN, J. (1993). 'Will Ottawa Protect Culture?', *Calgary Herald* (28 Dec.), B7.

POSNER, M. (1993). *Canadian Dreams: The Making and Marketing of Independent Films*. Vancouver: Douglas & McIntyre.

PRAGNELL, A. (1985). *Television in Europe: Quality and Values in a Time of Change*. Manchester: European Institute for the Media, Monograph 5.

PRINDLE, D. (1993). *Risky Business: The Political Economy of Hollywood*. Boulder, Colo.: Westview Press.

RABOY, M., BERNIER, I., SAUVAGEAU, F., and ATKINSON, D. (1994). 'Cultural Development and the Open Economy: A Democratic Issue and a Challenge to Public Policy', *Canadian Journal of Communication*, 19(3I4), special issue, 37–62.

REICH, R. (1990). 'Who Is Us?' *Harvard Business Review* (Jan.–Feb.): 53–65.

REMINGTON, R. (1987). 'No Spitting Image for PM', *Edmonton Journal* (12 Jan.): B4.

RENAUD, J., and DZIADUL, C. (1992). 'The TBI Primetime Programming Survey', *Television Business International* (May): 130–4.

——and LITMAN, B. (1985). 'Changing Dynamics of the Overseas Marketplace for Television Programming', *Telecommunications Policy* (Sept.): 245–61.

ROFEKAMP, J. (1987). 'The International Market'. in B. Hehner (ed.), *Making It: The Business of Film and Television Production in Canada*. Toronto: Academy of Canadian Cinema and Television, Doubleday Canada.

ROGERS, E., and ANTOLA, L. (1985). 'Telenovelas: A Latin American Success Story', *Journal of Commmunication*, 35(4): 24–35.

ROSEN, D. (1990). *Off-Hollywood: The Making and Marketing of Independent Films*. New York: Grove Weidenfeld.

ROSEN, S. (1981). 'The Economics of Superstars', *American Economic Review*, 71(5): 845–57.

ROWLAND, W., and TRACEY, M. (1990). 'Worldwide Challenges to Public Service Broadcasting', *Journal of Communication*, 40(2): 8–27.

RUBIN, S. (1992). *Reel Exposure: How to Promote Today's Motion Pictures*. Shelter Island, NY: Broadway Press.

RYAN, B. (1991). *Making Capital From Culture*, Berlin: de Gruyter.

SCHILLER, H. (1969). *Mass Communication and American Empire*. New York: August M. Kelley.

——(1971). *Mass Communication and American Empire*. Boston: Beacon.

——(1976). *Communication and Cultural Dominance*. White Plains, NY: International Arts & Sciences Press.

SCHLESINGER, P. (1986). 'Trading in Fictions: What Do We Know About British Television Imports and Exports?' *European Journal of Communication*, 1(3): 263–87.

SCHULL, C., and MORGAN, J. (1989). 'Who'll Be at the Forum and Why?' *Playback* (Toronto) (4 Sept.): 34.

SEPSTRUP, P. (1990). *Transnationalization of Television in Western Europe*. London: John Libby.

SHARPE, W. (1964). 'Capital Asset Prices: A Theory of Market Equilibrium Under Conditions of Risk', *Journal of Finance*, 19(4): 425–552.

SHERMAN, D. (1987). 'US Films Sweeping Over France', *Playback* (Toronto) (16 Nov.): 14, 23.

SINCLAIR, J. (1992). 'Media and Cultural Industries: An Overview', *CIRCIT Newsletter* (Aug.): 3–5.

——(1995). 'The Business of International Broadcasting: Cultural Bridges and Barriers', paper presented to the Communications Research Forum, Sidney, 19–20 Oct.

SMITH, A. (1992). 'Public Broadcasting in a Multi-Channel Europe', in A. Silj (ed.), *The New Television in Europe*. London: John Libbey, ch. 4.

SMITH, S., and SMITH, V. (1986). 'Successful Movies: A Preliminary Empirical Analysis', *Applied Economics*, 18: 501–7.

STAIGER, J. (1985). 'The Package-Unit System: Unit Management after 1955', in D. Bordwell, J. Staiger, and K. Thompson, *The Classical Hollywood Cinema: Film Style and Mode of Production to 1960*. New York: Columbia University Press.

STEINER, P. (1952). 'Program Patterns and Preferences, and the Workability of Competition in Radio Broadcasting', *Quarterly Journal of Economics*, 66: 194–223.

STIGLER, G. (1971). 'The Theory of Economic Regulation', *Bell Journal of Economics and Management Science*, 2(1): 3–21.

STIPP, H., and SCHIAVONE, N. (1990). 'Research at a Commercial Television Network: NBC 1990', *Marketing Research*, 2(3): 3–10.

STORPER, M. (1993). 'Flexible Specialization in Hollywood: A Response to Aksoy and Robins'. *Cambridge Journal of Economics*, 17: 479–84.

Stratavision (1985). *The structure and performance of the Canadian Film and Video Distribution Sector*. Prepared for Department of Communications, Govt. of Canada. Toronto: Stratavision.

*TBI Yearbook 95* (1995). London: FT Media & Telecoms.

Telefilm Canada (1992). *Action Plan 1991–92*. Montreal: Telefilm Canada.

*Television Business International* (1996). London: FT Media & Telecoms.

THOMAS, M. (1996). 'Financing Audiovisual Works in France and in Europe', *Columbia–VLA Journal of Law and the Arts*, 20(3): 495–520.

THOMPSON, K. (1985). *Exporting Entertainment: America in the World Film Market 1907–1934*. London: British Film Institute.

THROSBY, D. (1994). 'The Production and Consumption of the Arts: A View of Cultural Economics', *Journal of Economic Literature*, 23(1): 1–29.

TRACEY, M. (1985). 'The Poisoned Chalice? International Television and the Idea of Dominance', *Daedalus*, 114(4): 17–56.

——(1988). 'Popular Culture and the Economics of Global Television', *Intermedia*, 16(2): 9–29.

——(1993). 'A Taste of Money: Popular Culture and the Economics of Global Television', in E. Noam and J. Millonzi (eds.), *The International Market in Film and Television Programs*. Norwood, NJ: Ablex, 163–99.

——and REDAL, W. (1995). 'The New Parochialism: The Triumph of the Populist in the Flow of International Television', *Canadian Journal of Communication*, 20(3): 343–66.

TURNSTALL, J. (1977). *The Media Are American*. New York: Columbia University Press.

US Dept. of Commerce, Office of Business Economics, National Income Division. Annual figures.

US Trade Representative (1996). ' "Special 301" on Intellectual Property Rights', Fact Sheet, 30 Apr. 1996. [Online] Available: http://www.usitc.gov/ [access date 1996, 2 May].

VARIS, T. (1974). 'Global Traffic in Television', *Journal of Communication*, 24(1): 102–9.

——(1984). 'The International Flow of Television Programs', *Journal of Communication*, 34(1): 90–9.

*Video Age International.* (1990). 'Love That Yank Dollar . . . But Not Conditions That Go With It' (Feb.): 41–2.

WALLACE, W., SEIGERMAN, A., and HOLBROOK, M. (1993). 'The Role of Actors and Actresses in the Success of Films: How Much Is a Movie Star Worth?' *Journal of Cultural Economics*, 17 (June): 1–27.

WASKO, J. (1994). *Hollywood in the Information Age: Beyond the Silver Screen.* Cambridge: Polity Press.

WATERMAN, D. (1988). 'World Television Trade: The Economic Effects of Privatization and New Technology', *Telecommunications Policy* (June): 141–51; repr. in E. Noam and J. Millonzi (eds.), *The International Market in Film and Television Programs.* Norwood, NJ: Ablex, 59–82.

WATSON, W. (1989). 'Cross-subsidization and Canadian Culture', in H. Chartrand, C. McCaughey, and W. Hendon (eds.), *Cultural Economics 88: A Canadian Perspective.* Akron: University of Akron Press, 226–35.

WILDMAN, S. (1995). 'Trade Liberalization and Policy for Media Industries: A Theoretical Examination of Media Flows', *Canadian Journal of Communication*, 20(3): 367–88.

——and SIWEK, S. (1988). *International Trade in Films and Television Programs.* Washington, DC: American Enterprise Institute for Public Policy Research.

WILKINSON, K. (1996). 'Program Acquisition Decisionmaking in the Latin American Cultural-Linguistic Television Market', paper presented to International Communication Association 46th Annual Conference, 23–7 May, Chicago.

WIND, Y. (1978). 'Issues And Advances in Segmentation Research'. *Journal of Marketing Research*, 15 (Aug.): 317–37.

*Wired* (1997). San Francisco, Calif.: Wired Ventures.

WRIGHT, C. (1987). 'Co-productions, A Window on the World for Homegrown Talent', *Playback* (Toronto) (7 Sept.): 37–8.

WYATT, J. (1994). *High Concept: Movies and Marketing in Hollywood.* Austin: University of Texas Press.

YAQUB, K. (1996). *New Media.* Term paper for Manec 470, University of Alberta. Available at www.bus.ualberta.ca/khalidtmp/newmedia/.

# Index

*Index compiled by Frank Pert*

holt